The Pastor has Gorgeous Legs

The Pastor has Gorgeous Legs

A Memoir
of an Ordinary pastor on an Extraordinary journey
who met Exceptional people

Lynne C. Holden

AuthorHouse™
1663 Liberty Drive
Bloomington, IN 47403
www.authorhouse.com
Phone: 1-800-839-8640

First published by AuthorHouse 06/06/2011

ISBN: 978-1-4567-6535-4 (sc)
ISBN: 978-1-4567-6534-7 (dj)
ISBN: 978-1-4567-6533-0 (ebk)

Library of Congress Control Number: 2011906984

Printed in the United States of America

Contents

Part One

Part Two

Part Three

Part Four

PART ONE

Introduction

I am just an ordinary pastor. I have served two churches as their settled pastor, and I have been the transitional pastor (interim pastor) for three other churches. There has been nothing particularly out of the ordinary in terms of these pastorates. Most pastors of small churches will be able to relate to my story. Like most pastors, I am not a famous preacher or writer on the circuit tour. Matt Lauer of the *Today Show* is not interviewing me, nor has Oprah asked me to join her show. Like most pastors, I am not a college or seminary teacher, asked to lead retreats and speak at conventions. Most pastors like me are well educated. I have always harbored beliefs that I do have ideas and thoughts that I would like to share with seminarians about the "practical" ways of ministry, but I don't believe, at this point in my life's journey, that I will ever be an adjunct professor at a seminary or community college. Moreover, I have never been on television or the radio as an evangelist or guest "expert." No, I have simply served Christ, His church and His mission in quite ordinary ways, but, the journey has been far from ordinary, and I have met exceptional people along the way. These anecdotal Memoirs are a collection of my life's experiences, individually, and are also about the people who have motivated me, and influencing, to some extent, the direction that my life and my life's work has taken.

These essays are what I see in the "mirror of my mind". These are personal memories which may differ in details if another who may have shared in these stories told the story over. That is to be expected. I have not changed names or places. If a name has been changed I will tell you, Dear Reader.

There is nothing ordinary about being asked to share in people's lives, especially in the life changing events of marriage, birth, baptism, and the other countless celebrations of life, including celebrating the lives of those who have died. Each and every time that I have been involved in the sharing of these occasions has been extraordinary. I am sure that every pastor of every religious denomination would and could say the same.

You, Dear Reader, may wonder what the difference is between a Minister and a Pastor! Allow me to explain that I use the words interchangeably for myself. All Pastors are Ministers, but not all ministers are Pastors in the strictest use of the word. I call all Christians "ministers" because all Christians have the responsibilities of serving Christ, His Church and His mission where they live, work, play and pray.

There have been some unique experiences I would like to share as well as things that I have learned as a woman pastor which, in my humble opinion, have been extraordinary. I've always said, "Someday I'll write a book about the things people have said to me or situations I have found myself in while in the pastorate." This is that book!

The title is taken from a comment a man made to my colleague, the Reverend Newell Bishop, during my first year of ordained ministry. I had been called to serve as the student pastor of the First Baptist Church of North Stonington, CT commonly known as the Pendleton Hill Baptist Church. Following my graduation from Seminary and the retirement of the incumbent pastor, Reverend Richard (Dick) Mitchell, the church called me. I remember there was one negative vote for my call. It came from Farmer Hill. He said, "I've never had a woman in my pulpit and I don't intend to have one now!" Everyone loved Farmer Hill and I was distraught. Already I had lost a member! I cried on Dick's shoulder and he said, "Don't worry." Dick went on to tell me about how he had lost a member when he refused to shave off his beard and a parishioner told him he wasn't going to sit in the pews staring at a bearded man. Then Dick continued, "So, Lynne, we are even: I lost a member because I had a beard, you lost a member because you can't grow one." That was in 1983. I know I am much older now and I can tell this because my eyebrows are growing out of my chin and they are WHITE.

The first funeral I officiated at was for a former Connecticut State Senator. I got to know "Charlie" over the year during which I was the student pastor. His home was just down the road from the church, and I enjoyed our visits. I can still recall the smell of his bread and butter pickles that he was famous for making. His funeral was an enormous affair. Most of North Stonington came, along with various state officials and dignitaries. The little church was bulging at the seams. The horseshoe balcony was full and there were people in the foyer flowing through the front door and out onto the grounds. After the burial we gathered in the church basement for refreshments. Newell Bishop came up to me and said, "See that fellow over there. He told me you have gorgeous legs." I looked at Newell somewhat bewildered because I had never had any sort of compliment like that from anyone, so I just said, "Well, you go tell him he is welcome to come to church any Sunday and look at them."

Fast forward to May 2, 2005. I was sitting with my *D*ad outside the nursing office at the Overlook Nursing Home in Pascoag, Rhode Island. We were there for his family conference. As we were waiting in the hall for our turn to meet with the staff and administrator, *D*ad said to me, "You look nice in your skirt." "Thank you," I said. Then he said, "You should pull your skirt up ever so slightly and allow your legs to show more . . . you know, you have gorgeous legs." At 89 the man was still looking! Dad died three days later. What a lovely memory of our last true conversation.

Then, on Mother's Day 2005 my oldest grandson, Robert, who was 5 at the time, made me a card. His mother wrote as he dictated. My card read: "Happy Mother's Day. I love you. I like your legs."

So the verdict is in! From a stranger, a father and a grandson—the pastor has gorgeous legs.

Girls Can't Do That!

My Dad always loved to say, "Lynne was a great football player but she quit once she realized the boys were tackling her for other reasons other than wanting the ball." I don't remember that, but Dad seemed to. I do remember loving to play football. When I was 10 years old, I asked for a football for Christmas and I received one. It was white leather with a black stripe on each end. The leather had little pockmarks that got dirty and I hated that; I wanted it to look good. Thus, the football would often get washed. The laces were cowhide, a beautiful dark brown. What a lovely football. I could throw it half way down the street and watch it spiral right into the arms of my friend Bill. He was two years older than I and his sister, Arlene, was my best friend. She didn't like football too much. She didn't think girls should do that.

The Christmas that I received my football was the Christmas my maternal grandparents were coming for the day. My maternal grandfather was a physician, and he was a very important person, at least in his eyes. I knew that my mother was afraid of him; I certainly was. All the grandkids were afraid of Grandfather Mellott. However, with all due respect, his patients must have loved him because at his funeral there were five rooms at the funeral parlor filled with flowers and a steady stream of visitors. My mother would say, "He was an angel abroad and a devil at home." His daughter, my Aunt Joanne, told me once, "Dad was so busy minding everyone else's business in town, he didn't have time to mind anything at home." Thesc "things" I was too young to know, but I do remember we were afraid of him, and Mother warned me just before my grandparents were to arrive for Christmas dinner, "Now Lynne, when your grandfather gets here, please hide that football. Please don't mention it at all, because you know that he will say, 'Girls Can't Do That!'" I now know that

Mother was afraid of what grandfather would say to her, not me, about the appropriateness of giving a 10-year-old girl a football. I played football until I was 13 but then the light came on and suddenly I realized "Girls can't do that."

My mother was raised in a very austere environment and always looming over her like a shadow were these words, "What would the neighbors think?" There were very few career options for women in my mother's day; she could train to be a nurse, a secretary or a teacher. My mother, like her mother, went to Indiana State Teachers College in Indiana, Pennsylvania, where she studied to become an elementary school teacher. My mother loved being a teacher. She enjoyed teaching so much that she even took a summer course at Duke University, which in those days of economic stress, was unheard of her first year out of college. She taught elementary students for three years. Then she married my Dad and that was the end of her teaching career. Married women in those days were not allowed to teach!

I tell you these things, Dear Reader, to set the stage of what was appropriate and what was not appropriate for a young girl to dream about when she was growing up. I, like my mother and her mother, could train to be a nurse, a secretary, a teacher and by my early adulthood, we could add, airline stewardess. I didn't want to do any of those things. I had felt the call and wanted to be a preacher. I was in my teens and had never met a woman preacher. I was told many times by my pastor, "Girls can't do that." My guidance counselor in high school said, "Girls can't do that." My parents said, "Girls can't do that." I struggled with this disconnect for at least five years. I knew God wanted me to be a preacher and yet no one else thought I could or should be a preacher.

I was 13 when I went off to Camp Jumonville, a Methodist camp and conference center about 50 miles from home, in Uniontown, Pennsylvania. I was the one who chose to go to this camp. I had gone, the year before, to a co-ed weekly camp session and even though I loved the singing and the great outdoors, the campfires and the other girls I met, I didn't have that much fun. I had "some" fun, but whenever I would show up for a baseball game, the boys said, "Girls can't do that," and I was told to sit on the grass and cheer or go find something else to do. I would find something else to do. So, that year, when I was 13, I asked to go to the all-girls session of camp.

In the all-girls camp, there may not have been boys to dress for or talk to or have them make fun of us, yet we did have to dress for dinner. We were told we could only bring two crinolines for our big felt circle shirts; yes, some girls had a poodle on the skirt. Mine did not, and I only owned one crinoline. These "poodle" skirts were popular at that time, in the 50's, but are no longer popular, and, in fact, are now looked upon as rather old fashioned. We, on the other hand, at that time, thought that we were the epitome of fashion. I find it hard to think that those skirts, shirtwaist dresses, and cardigan sweater sets are now called "vintage clothing."

Our days were fairly structured with arts and crafts, morning and evening chapel, morning Bible Study, recreation in the afternoon and some free time before we had to dress for dinner. One afternoon I went up the hill (some would call this hill a small mountain) to sit under the famous, gigantic cross. It is still there. On the Jumonville website [1]one can read about the cross, built in 1950, a cross of steel 60 feet high standing on a concrete base six feet tall on Dunbar's Knob, which itself is 2,480 feet above sea level. Lying in the grass with the shadow of the cross looming above me, I felt very close to God. I often tried to go to this sacred place, which the Celtics call, "a thin place;" that is, a place where heaven and earth meet. My thin place at the age of 13 was at the base of a 60 foot gleaming white, steel cross which could be seen from miles away. And it was then and there, that I knew God wanted me to be a preacher. How did I know? God did not speak to me in any audible language. I didn't have a vision of Jesus with out-stretched arms calling me to follow him. I had no female role models. All I can say is that I knew to my very core that I had just been asked to commit my life to God and to prepare myself to be a preacher.

That night at the campfire the typical altar call was made. All those who wished to dedicate themselves to "full time Christian service" were invited to come forward and I went. At that time when I was a girl of 13, "fulltime Christian Service" meant I was coming forward for all to see that I wanted to be a missionary or work in a church in the Sunday school. I was too immature to know that there was a third option and that was to be a pastor's wife! I committed my life to God that night! And then I told my camp counselor that I was planning on being a preacher and she

---

[1] http://www.thecrossphoto.com/The_White_Cross_located_at_Jumonville_in_Hopwood_PA.htm

said, "Girls can't do that!" "But," I said, "I know God wants me to be a preacher. God told me this afternoon." And you guessed it, she said, "My dear, you must have heard wrong because Girls can't do that!!"

When I went home I told my parents I had dedicated my life to God, they didn't seem too pleased. In their mind I was all excited about being a missionary and I said, "No not that. I'm going to be a preacher." And they condescendingly said, "Girls can't do that." I told my pastor of the West View Methodist Church that I had dedicated my life to Christ and that I was going to be a preacher. He was just brutal in his pronouncement that Girls do not do that! Then he said no school would accept me to be trained as a preacher. It was years later, far too many years to make a difference, when I discovered that the Methodist Church had ordained a woman as early as 1880.

What did I know? By the time I had graduated from high school in 1960, I had been told so many times that girls are not to be preachers that I had made these ideas my own and had accepted them. Sort of.

Following graduation from high school, I headed off to West Virginia Wesleyan College to major in Christian Education. I had come to the blunt realization that I must have misheard God on that mountain top. My vocational call must be Christian Education. It pleased my parents! My grandmother Caughey was thrilled, and she confided in me that she was hoping I would go to Moody Institute or Bob Jones University in South Carolina. And my pastor was pleased! Everyone was happy except—guess who? I knew that Christian education was not my true calling. One semester into the program and I knew I did not want to pursue a degree in Christian Education. I had fallen in love with Biology and Dr. George Rossbach never told me, "*Y*ou can't study biology because you are a girl."

I was called to be a preacher at the tender age of 13, and I honestly tried to live out that call. It wouldn't be for another 27 years when that call could be realized. But, Dear Reader, that is another chapter in this story.

Lynne and Ted 1946

Early Christian Formation

Over the years I have been asked, "Are You Saved?" I've seen signs on the side of barns and other inappropriate places proclaiming, "Jesus Saves." I could be very sarcastic and turn around ask: "Am I saved? Have I been put aside, kept, hoarded, or salted away? Does Jesus accumulate, collect, conserve, and store?" I saw another sign which read, "Jesus Saves-Green stamps." No one saves Green stamps anymore. Jesus does rescue. One's Spiritual Life can be salvaged, changed, set free, and liberated by his or her adopting a life in Christ. St. Paul speaks of freedom from sin, and I do as well. I also mean when I say I was "saved" by Christ that I am unbound not only from sin, but from any and all things that would try to limit my individuality, my potential for growth. I mean I have been saved from that which would prevent me from being the woman God has created me to be. Yes, I not only admit, but I proclaim that I am saved. Can I pick a day and time and announce to the world that I was rescued from the pit of deprivation by acknowledging Jesus as my Lord and Savior. Yes and No. Yes, I was, along with all of creation, saved on Good Friday over 2000 years ago. As to the precise day and time in my life, I can't think of one day or one time. I think there are and have been lots of days and times when I knew that without the love of God, through Christ, in my life, I would be doomed. I know what some Christians mean by a "testimony" about when I was "saved" but I refuse to speak in that language. After all, it is simply a different style of speaking about being a Christian.

I was brought up in a Christian home. The entire family regularly went to the West View Methodist Church, and after we moved, we went to the Ingomar Methodist Church. As early as I can recall I knew some of the Bible stories such as Noah's Ark, and contrary to public opinion, Noah's wife was not named Joan. We learned about and studied the major characters of the Old Testament in Sunday school. I recall making dioramas, using hand puppets, enjoying an assortment of arts and crafts, acting in plays, coloring our "hand-outs" and using an array of methods and materials that the Sunday school teachers used in that golden age of Christian Education during the 1950s. The church was a major social, as well as religious focal point, growing up in Western Pennsylvania immediately following WWII and through the Eisenhower years. Everyone went to church. There was a great divide between Protestants and Catholics but most people seemed to be attached to some form or expression of Christianity as I was growing up.

My paternal grandmother was instrumental and influential in my Christian formation. She would read the Bible to me and have me memorize psalms and various other passages. It pleased her that I could memorize scripture and I liked pleasing her. She always told me that I was going to be a great witness for Jesus. I believed her.

Mother read Bible stories to me along with *Heidi*, *Snow White*, the *Mother Goose* Rhymes, *Black Beauty* and countless other books. She taught me the love of reading. When I had mastered the art of reading I was able to pick out my own books, and every night I would read until mother would call out, "Time to turn out the lights now." Each day's reading would include a small passage of the Bible from a child's devotional.

Prayers were always said before meals and before bedtime. Traditional prayers were taught to us such as "Now I lay me down to sleep . . . God bless Mommie, God bless Daddy" and if I really didn't want to go to sleep I might "God Bless" everyone and everything I knew—stalling for time. We knew the Grace: "God is great, God is good, now we thank Him for our food . . .", but Dad never said the grace when we had a casserole. He was a meat and potato man!

So I can say that my early Christian foundation was begun at home and encouraged in the same way one is encouraged to learn to walk, read, write and do one's numbers. It was part of growing up. This is what one did in our household. It was expected of us—it was part of "growing up." The love of God was cultivated in us in the same way parents try to cultivate manners, values and priorities in any child's life. To insist that one must have a "Damascus Road" (Acts 9: 1-9) style encounter with God or Christ as the only way to be "saved" is, in my opinion, misguided and often harmful.

Consequently it was not unusual for me to go to a Christian camp and at the tender age of 13 to know that I wanted to belong to Christ forever, that is, for Jesus to be a part of me, and for me to be a part of Him, and that I wanted to be a preacher. What was unusual I came to be told and to believe was that God didn't talk to girls about being preachers and ministers of the Faith, or at least that is what my parents, my grandmother, my pastor and my Sunday school teachers told me. It would take almost 27 years before I had what traditional Christian's label, "The Call." Yet, after almost three decades of serving Christ, His church and His mission I still have some Christians tell me to my face and speak to others: "She isn't saved, she doesn't know Christ, and she won't give her testimony!" Amazing! This form of Christianity is arrogant, rude and judgmental. It is this type of Christianity from which I have been released, rescued, set free, unbound, yes, **Saved.**

Elementary and Junior High School

I think, Dear Reader, that it is important for me to tell you about my earliest memories and recollections of school and early adolescence before I tell you about my "Second Call" which resulted in my admission to the Ordained Ministry. During these early years of my life, I flourished as we hope all children might do as they mature. I continued to be involved in my church. During my college years, like so many young people looking for their own way, I left the church, the rituals, the ceremonies, and I abandoned my faith and the philosophy of Christianity to the chagrin of my pastor, but even more so, to my parents. Have patience. I will tell you more about that decision and the return of my faith in the Lord in the following chapters.

I went to Quail Elementary School in North Hills, Pa. I walked from Renton Ave, over the street car bridge, past the entrance to the park with the public swimming pool, and along a busy highway to the school. That is all I can recall for directions. There was a huge horse chestnut tree along the highway, and I loved collecting the "buckeyes" in the fall. I learned if you save the "buckeyes" in your dresser drawer too long, they get bugs, and as fast as I would save them, my mother would throw them away.

In the fifth grade we were permitted to buy street car passes which saved me the worry of that bridge. I was appointed a street car monitor. We had white belts that crossed over our chests, in typical Sam Brown fashion, and wrapped around our waists with a very impressive badge worn on the belt over the right shoulder. I liked being a street car monitor. I'm not so sure my younger brother, Ted, liked his sister telling him what to do at the bus stop or on the bus, but brothers never like big sisters telling them what to do, especially in front of the other kids, and I was very good at it.

I remember I had Miss Bruggerman as a first and second grade teacher. My mother liked her and even invited her to dinner several times. Please note the "Miss." It was customary in "those" days to invite "single" teachers to the home. I'm not so sure I thought it was fun to have my teacher over for dinner. I do know I thought Miss Bruggerman was a nice teacher . . . except that times when she punished me. This is what happened.

There was a cloak room attached to the classroom . . . . a large room with a sink and hooks for our jackets and a shelf for our lunch boxes. (Yes, in those days there were no hot lunch cafeterias—we carried our lunch to school.) Our boots rested on a little rack under the coat hooks. I was sent to the cloak room once as punishment, and I have no recollection now as to what I had done. While I was in the cloakroom, I found the teacher's handbag and took out her lipstick and proceeded to try to put some on. I guess I figured no one would be able to tell. But, alas, Miss Bruggerman knew, having taken one look at me when she came in to let me out. I can only recall that she was angry (think "livid") and I was in trouble at home as well. The next time I had to be disciplined (I have no idea about why these disciplines were necessary) I had to sit under Miss Bruggerman's desk, and there was nothing to amuse me there except to stare at Miss Bruggerman's very large legs! Maybe she thought that that was additional punishment!!!

In the fourth grade my teacher was Miss Hartman. I recall she was very tall, and since I was beginning to shoot up she seemed to take a special interest in me regarding my height. I liked her, but I didn't like her fussing about my height. She was like mother: "Stand up straight, now!" "Be proud of your height." Fortunately, I wasn't the tallest person in the room; my friend Penny was the tallest person in the class. As I remember, Penny was also very thin and had very beautiful long brown hair that hung over her shoulders. I thought she was beautiful. I wasn't thin. My hair was in a bob; mouse brown with a Miss Clairol permanent, I never liked it. People would say about me, "She's a big girl, isn't she?" Today when I look at photos of that period I don't see myself as a "big" girl, i.e. fat, but I grew up with the sense that I was a tall, fat girl, an attitude that has followed me all of my life.

The best part of 4th grade was my addiction to reading a biography series published by Westminster Press. I know the publisher because recently my friend Sally Nuss, a children's librarian, found me a copy of the series. When I held that musty orange covered book in my hands, I remembered the hours of enjoyment I had reading each and every book of that series my 4th grade classroom had on the shelves. I have always enjoyed reading. I read for the knowledge. I read for the fun. I read as an escape. I believe that once a child learns the joy of reading, then that child can go anyplace and do anything, at least for the time the child is engaged with that book. It was in the 4th grade that my love of reading began to flourish, and I wanted to read to mother. Up to this time, she read to me every night and once we got to chapter books, I would wait all day until we could snuggle in bed and mother would read the next chapter of *Lassie*, or *Nancy Drew*, or the *Hardy Boys*. As a fourth grader, I didn't need to wait for bedtime to read; I could read anytime, anywhere. As I said before, almost every night, mother would come to my bedroom door and say, "Time to turn out the lights now." Even today, it is very hard for me to go to sleep without reading for a little while.

I took the street car to Samuel Hamilton Junior High School. We didn't have Middle Schools then. "Sam Ham", like Quail School might not even be in existence anymore. In any case, we went to junior high for grades 7, 8 and 9. I was in the band, playing clarinet.

I don't recall much of junior high except that I enjoyed the band and that in the 8th grade I memorized the Periodic Table. I learned 100 elements, and I remember standing in front of my eighth grade science class and repeating all the elements, giving the name, abbreviation, and atomic number. Today, I can recall the abbreviations of most of the common elements (nitrogen, sodium, chlorine, gold, silver, aluminum, iron, etc) but I don't remember their atomic numbers. I certainly would not be able to list 100 elements today. Even then, I was attracted to science and even today, I wonder if my fascination with science, chemistry, elements, biology, etc. had, or might have had, some tie in or connection to my Faith—at that time in my life.

It is not important that I learned the Periodic Table. It was important that I was teaching my mind to memorize, organize and recall. My mother told me I was memorizing and repeating poems and songs to her guests and our relatives when I was two and three years old. All through school I was able to memorize a "piece" and stand up in front of the class and recite it flawlessly. In Sunday school, we had to memorize scripture verses. Today, it is very hard for me to memorize much. I find myself forgetting simple things: names of people I know well and points I want to make during a sermon. There was a period of time at the Greenville Baptist

Church that I delivered all my sermons without a manuscript. I may have had a few notes in the margin of my Bible, but in reality I was speaking without notes. Today, I use a manuscript. I feel free to deviate from it and often do, as the spirit moves me. But the manuscript is a comfort to me because I have these mind blanks or mind blocks; I call them mind farts, and I am at a complete loss, sometimes, of what I want to say. This happens in the public forum and in private conversations. Yet, I am glad I was able to excel at memorization and it helped me hone my skills as a public speaker and as a debater for the team at West Virginia Wesleyan College.

I believe children need to learn how to memorize little poems at first, then major pieces like the Gettysburg Address and the Preamble to the Constitution. I wonder if my grandchildren will ever be able to repeat the 23rd psalm or psalm 100. What translation will they use? It is of no real importance, the translation they use, but rather—will they have buried in their hearts and minds pieces of scripture that will come to them in times of joy and in times of sorrow? Will they have hidden in their hearts words of comfort, words of encouragement, words of celebration which they will live and model? Time will tell.

1719 Renton Avenue
(The early years 1946-1957)

I can't be sure how many years we lived at 1719 Renton Ave, in the North Hills of Pittsburgh, PA, but I recall nine because I attended the Quail School for my elementary years and Samuel Hamilton Junior High for grades seven through nine. I remember how much I anticipated entering the West View High School, only to learn in my freshman year at Sam Ham that we would be moving and I would attend North Allegheny High School. Bummer!

But let me take you back to my growing up years on Renton Ave. I have several outstanding memories of that time. I remember that all the kids in the neighborhood, including my brother, Ted, and my sister, Nancy, loved the week before Halloween. During that week mother would allow us to go out after dinner and "trick" our neighbors. I have no idea why mother allowed us to cook up such mischief because she was a very strict mother and a woman of no nonsense. We did not smash pumpkins, throw toilet paper around or soap windows, although there were some kids that did do that. We had pea shooters; long plastic straws designed to hold white navy beans. We would pelt the windows of those neighbors who had given us a hard time all summer. We would hide behind a tree or bush and aim for the windows of our neighbor next door. Ping! Ping! Ping, the beans would hit the windows. Old Mr. What's—His—Name (I can't remember) would come to the door and yell for us to "Cut it out! Go home!" We would be very still and wait for him to go back into the house and he would turn out the porch light and we would start again. Immediately, the door was flung open and he would be yelling again, "I'll call the cops. Go home you little monsters." Still we would persist. No cops ever came. Eventually, we would grow tired of harassing him, or we would resort to ringing his door bell and running to hide. I recall one time when I snuck up to ring his doorbell and suddenly I was soaking wet. He had been waiting for me and when I got to the door, he quietly opened the window on the second floor above the door, and the minute I touched that bell, he opened the window and poured a bucket of water on me. That ended that night of "tricking" neighbors. I was the one tricked!

There were other neighbors who bore the brunt of our pea shooters and doorbell ringing but never Mrs. Ellenberger's home. We liked Mrs. Ellenberger. And she liked us. Whenever our baseball would go in her yard, she allowed us to fetch it. She never kept it like the neighbor across the street from her place. That couple did not want us playing baseball in front of their yard. We only had the street to play in; there were no parks or ball fields on or near Renton Ave. So the street itself was our park where we rode our bikes, played baseball, tag football, kick the can, and dodge ball. Whenever any ball went into this nasty neighbor's yard, and we were not fast enough to retrieve it, we lost it. Once Mr. What's-His-Name came out and yelled at us and we were not very polite, I will admit it. Then Mrs. What's-Her-Name came out and yelled at her husband, "You come in here right now! Your ice cream is getting cold." My brother and I still laugh over that exchange some fifty years later.

My Dad loved to tell the story of Mrs. Ellenberger's daughter who married and the couple moved into Mrs. Ellenberger's house. The couple's name was Batty. Mrs. Ellenberger always did her wash on Mondays. She, like everyone else in the neighborhood, hung her clothes on the line to dry; sheets folded in half and clipped to the outermost line. That way, the underwear, bedroom clothes and personals were hung on the inner lines and the sheets offered some sense of privacy. For weeks after the newly-weds moved in, Mrs. Ellenberger did her laundry and the couple's laundry, and each week she noticed there were no pajamas or nighties from the Battys. She finally could not contain herself any longer and so she asked her daughter why there were no pajamas or nighties, to which her daughter said, "Well mother, we don't use pajamas, we sleep in the nude." From that time on, Mrs. Ellenberger hung a pair of pajamas and a nightie on her clothes line on the street side of the sheets for all the neighbors to see.

The Ellenbergers lived next door to the Forbes. The Forbes had one child named Denny: Denny Forbes. He was the same age as my sister,

Nancy. Denny tried to hang around with her, but she wasn't keen on Denny. He was short and round, a little boy with black, thick framed glasses and a lisp. His father made his living by supplying schools with dissecting materials: frogs, cats, white rats and fetal pigs. He did all his work in their basement, so the entire house smelled like formaldehyde and so did Denny Forbes. We were very curious about the goings-on in the basement, a sort of bizarre fascination. We would peak in the windows and see cats hanging upside down. The morbidity of Denny Forbes' basement was as close to being terrifying as any horror film or the "Ride and Laff" fun house at the West View amusement park. We never let our house cat out for fear of Mr. Forbes.

One afternoon when I was older, my friend Arlene Fisher and I, along with the neighborhood gang, were playing ball, as usual, at the end of the street by the Ellenbergers, the Forbes and the "enemy couple." As usual, one of the balls went into their yard, and the police appeared. The policeman sent everyone home. He looked at Arlene and me and said, "Where do you two live?" I answered and pointed, "Down the street." "Well," he said, "you just head that way." And we did. Until I said to Arlene, "Why should we have to go home? We weren't doing anything wrong. Let's turn around and if the policeman asks us where we live, we can say we are going to your house." Of course, Arlene didn't live in that direction. So we boldly headed back to where the policeman stood, and we announced we were going to Arlene's home instead, and he said, "Oh no you aren't." And he marched us both down the street. When we got to 1719 Renton Avenue the policeman walked us both to the front door and rang the bell. When mother came to the door she had horror written all over her face. Here was her eldest child being accompanied by a police officer to her front door. What would the neighbors think?!! She sent Arlene home with some angry rebuff, thanked the officer and sent him off and then looked at me and said, "Young lady, never have I been more embarrassed, to think a police officer had to walk you down the street and everyone could see you. You go to your room and stay there till morning." Mother and Dad were planning on going out that night and Grandmother Caughey had come to baby-sit. Mother told grandmother, in no uncertain words, that I was being punished and that I was to stay in my room. "Was that clear!?" And off my parents went for the evening. At some point, Grandmother came and got me, (or I went to her, I'm not sure) and we sat together on the green glider on the porch, just being together. She never scolded.

She never asked questions. We just quietly rocked back and forth on that glider, holding hands and waiting for the sun to set. As you can imagine, when mother came home and found us peaceful on the glider, she was none too pleased, to put it mildly. And that is the story of my first and only encounter with the police, well aside from a speeding ticket or two.

Some of our friends' names were Arlene and Bill Fisher. Bill was older than I, and I liked him some. Kim Wilson was also older and I loved him, lots . . . to no avail. There were the Browns, the Mehews, and the Schnoffers whose dog tore me apart when I was six, and I still am leery of dogs that I don't know. And there were Joyce and Butchy Krapp. My brother likes to say, "If I had a name like Butchy Krapp, I would change it. (and then he waits and smiles) I'd change it to Bill."

The Caughey Family 1954
L to R Ed and Helen Caughey
L to R Martha 2, Nancy 7, Ted 10 and Lynne 12

When the Saints Come Marching In North Allegheny High School 1957-1960

Our theme song for the marching band at all football games was, "When the Saints Come Marching In." We took great pride in how we presented ourselves on the football field during half time. We looked good! Black and gold uniformed musicians keeping perfect pitch, time and movements on the 50 yard line gave me much enjoyment during my high school years. We would perform from memory; that is without music sheets attached to our instruments. I played clarinet, the "licorice stick" as it was known at that time. Our white bucks were brushed and dusted with white powder so that our footwear sparkled. We looked and sounded great! I loved our band uniforms and enjoyed those occasions when the band was scheduled to take the bus to an away game and we were allowed to wear our uniforms to classes. Girls were allowed to wear trousers! They were black with a bold gold stripe down the outside seam of the leg. Every other day in the "50's, the most common mode of female attire was a skirt and sweater set or a dress. If we wore a dress, the dress might be a sack dress, an A-line or a shirtwaist. My mother made all of my dresses. I can still recall the feeling of her fingernail marking the middle of my calf where she measured the hem of my skirts and dresses. That was what we wore to school. On the weekends we used to wear saddle shoes, you know, the white shoes with a brown leather strip that ran across the middle of the shoe, and we used to "borrow" our fathers' old dress shirts and wear them without tucking them in so that the tails hung out the back. This was high fashion for us, and we would wear jeans if our parents would allow it. This was sort of the beginning of the feminine "revolution." I have a male friend, now in his late 70's, remark that "a skirt and sweater on a woman is the sexiest clothes that she could wear." I was rarely in a skirt and sweater set!

I suppose that all students of High School whether in the 50s or 90s or into the 21st century have similar ways of grouping themselves. We had the "jocks," the "nerds," the "brains," the "preps," the various cliques among the girls and the "rebels" with their D.A. hair styles. For you, Dear Reader, the D.A. stands for Duck's Ass. When my brother, Ted, came home one day with a D.A. hair style, his blond hair greased back into a point in the back (in the shape of a duck's tail) and the top of his head cut close and flat, our father had one of his few rages. He said he wasn't going to have a "greaser" in his house! Anyone who tried to look like Cookie in the TV show "*77 Sunset Strip*" or that "gyrating" rock and roller, Elvis Presley, was not going to be the role model for Dad's son. Period!

I had a group of friends in high school that belonged to the Y-Teens, a group sponsored by the Young Christian Women's Association (YWCA). Our adult adviser and leader was Hope King. We always had someone in our group who had access to a car so this group of gals traveled together in our own little gang. We would go to have hamburgers at Eat and Park. We would pack as many girls as we could in a car and go to the Drive In movies on Friday nights. Dad called these places "passion pits." And he was correct. Those in our class who had coupled off and were "going steady" would often be seen at the Drive In and subject themselves to our smiles and nods, and seeing them there would start our gang talking about them. I remember the stories—some were made up, but most had an element of truth, even though they were grossly exaggerated. I never dated in high school.

Most of the girls in the Y-Teens were like me: decent students but not the "brains." And not the social butterflies. We were not of the IN group of girls, the BIG clique where everyone was cute, stylish, had boyfriends, and made the rest of us feel like second class citizens. We all wore the same styles of cuffed bobby socks with saddle shoes or penny loafers. We all had matching cardigan sweater sets. If we wore a blouse, the sleeves were short and cuffed, and we finished the look with a scarf around our neck. The blouse complimented our wool skirts which had a slit up the back and the length of the skirt was at the middle of our calf. We all wore our hair in pony tails or shoulder length "page boy" style. Yet, somehow, I always felt out of place and very different from most of the girls in High

School. Thank God for the Y-Teens and our advisor, Hope King. With them I felt at home, sort of my family away from home. My closest friends during my sophomore year were girls who were seniors and who had the leadership positions in the Y-Teens. When they graduated I felt very alone. I didn't have any close friends in my class. I did have the band members with whom I shared a common interest, and I was active in the Methodist Youth Fellowship (MYF) at the local and regional levels. These two groups gave me a place to be and as far as the Youth group was concerned, a social atmosphere in which I felt comfortable.

Something that we did in the public high school that I attended, which would not happen today, was a little unusual. It was permitted that once a week during the last period of the day anyone who wished to could leave the school and walk up the hill to attend religious classes held at the Lutheran or Catholic Church. I'm not sure how many students went because they desired a religious education or if it was a chance to leave school and lollygag their way up the hill. I enjoyed the time and the entire experience. There was never any lollygagging coming down the hill because we had buses to catch.

Our Senior Prom was held in the gym and the reception was held in the cafeteria. Our Prom was a far cry from the elaborate proms of today which are often held at fine hotels or country clubs, and the couples arrive by stretch limos and have all-night parties. Today, the boys are dressed in tuxedos, and the girls are often attired in very expensive gowns. In our time, i.e. the 50's, many boys wore suits, and neckties, and the girls . . . . Well, read on. One thing that WAS done in our time was the presentation of a corsage by the boys to their dates, and the girls wore them with great pride. My mother made my prom dress, a lovely blue taffeta gown with a full skirt that required several crinoline petticoats. It was not unusual for most girls to be wearing gowns that their mother had made, or one that had been worn before by an older sister or relative. My "date" was a boy I knew from the Methodist Youth Fellowship who was on the same council that I served. He lived on the other side of Pittsburgh. Bill was also going to West Virginia Wesleyan as we had both been accepted as early admissions in the first semester of our high school senior year. He was going to major in pre-ministerial classes, the classes I wanted to take but could not because, you got it, I was a girl. Since mother had said, "You really should try and find a date for the prom," I asked Bill and he was a good sport and took me. He wore a tuxedo! He brought me a corsage made up of white roses and tied in a blue ribbon to match my gown. He was so sweet to make me feel as if this was a REAL date. He was my one and only "date" in high school.

The academics of high school kept me occupied. I loved biology. I especially enjoyed public speaking, and my English teacher thought I was quite gifted in that direction, so I entered several speaking contests and was chosen to give one of the four graduation addresses. Graduation was held on the football field. I was happy to graduate and I looked forward to a new adventure at college. Aside from the activities of MYF, Y-Teens and the Band, I didn't really enjoy High School, so I was ready to move on. Little did I know that college wouldn't be much better, but that is another story!

High School Senior 1960

West Virginia Wesleyan College Buckhannon, West Virginia 1960-1964

I was excited about going off to college. My three years at North Allegheny High School rotated around the Y-Teens, the Band and the Methodist Youth Fellowship (MYF). I held local and regional offices in both the Y-Teens and the MYF. These activities made High School bearable.

In my junior year of High School I had applied for early acceptance at West Virginia Wesleyan College (WVWC). The pressures that so many of my peers were feeling in their senior year did not apply to me. I knew where I was going, what I would be studying, and what my major would be. I knew I would be majoring in Christian Education (CE), and I couldn't wait to put High School behind me.

The campus of WVWC was picture book beautiful. It still is. Majestic old trees lined the walk-ways. The buildings were red brick and white columned. The lawns were manicured as were the gardens. The campus was nestled in the valley of the surrounding Appalachian mountain range, and it would be the setting for my next four years. It was a very beautiful and scenic place.

My parents and I arrived in the fall of 1960 after a four hour drive from Pittsburgh to the Agnes Howard Hall, my freshman year dormitory. I had signed up with a girl from the regional offices of the MYF to be my roommate. I don't recall how or why we changed roommates during the first semester, but I recall I then shared the room with a girl from Cuba who was unable to get back to her homeland because of the "Bay of Pigs" episode. Our room was large and we shared the bathroom with the room next to us, the bathroom dividing the rooms. It was an older dorm but it was a pleasant room.

What was not pleasant was to discover all the rules. When I applied to Wesleyan I was interested in the Christian Education (CE) department, since that was the only avenue available to me if I wanted to continue to be in "full time Christian service," the term Methodists used for anyone interested in serving the church or being a missionary. I knew I wanted to be a pastor, but I was told early on that women could not be pastors and would not be accepted into the pre-ministerial programs at any of the Methodist based colleges. What did I know? I listened to my pastor and decided to pursue CE, but in my heart of hearts, I wasn't really happy about this. I thought it very unfair to be discriminated against because of gender. Still, there I was at Wesleyan enrolled in the CE program and now I was faced with the rules.

In 1960, these were the rules all women had to obey as freshmen at WVWC.

1. All Freshmen women were to be in the dorm by 9 p.m. Freshmen women were allowed 3 late nights with proper excuses per semester.
2. No male visitors were allowed beyond the lobby except on moving in and moving out day and then one would yell, "Man on the floor."
3. All women dressed for dinner: i.e. nylons and heels. No slacks could be worn except for gym, band, or in the privacy of one's dorm room.
4. Men could not wear jeans or sneakers to dinner, they needed a tie and jacket.
5. There was to be no public display of affection. Hand holding was OK. The school did sponsor dances at the Benedum Community Center.
6. Mandatory attendance at the weekly chapel service held in the auditorium. The present day Chapel had not been built.
7. Lights out by 11p.m.

Infractions of these rules meant that your 3 late night privileges were revoked. If these were all used, the next level of discipline was that you were not to leave the dorm over the week-end, a form of being grounded.

I hated the rules. As sophomores, juniors and seniors we progressed upward from a 9 p.m. curfew for reporting to the dorm, so that by the time we were seniors we could stay out until 11p.m. and we had 6 late nights per semester. Still, we were being told when we had to be back in the dorm and when lights were to be out. As a High School student, my parents trusted me to be where I said I would be at any given time, to the time when I would come home. When I said I would come home, I would be home and so, at home I did not live under this type of restrictive "rules." There I was in college, 18 years old, mature and responsible and I was suddenly faced with rules which made no sense to me. The boys could stay at the library until closing while the freshmen girls had to be back at the dorm by 9 p.m. I didn't understand why freshmen women could not also study at the library until its closing at 11p.m.

I didn't like the dress code. At home, when I was in High School I wore skirts to class but once I got home I was in my blue jeans. I lived in my jeans. Mother dressed for dinner every night. Dad took off his suit jacket to eat but he too "dressed" for dinner. I didn't dress for dinner except on Sundays.

The rule of no public display of affection didn't affect me. I didn't have anyone in the four years of college with whom to display or not display affection. I was considered by my peers to be a devoted and academic student who, as one friend said, "she doesn't suffer fools easily."

I look back upon those 4 years of college and what sticks out in my mind are the rules. And the rules so irritated me that I became rebellious. I was never rebellious during High School. My parents treated me with respect and the respect was mutual. I felt belittled, discriminated against, and disrespected by the college rules, as if we were not capable of making wise decisions for ourselves because we were of the feminine gender.

Rebellion: I took up drinking. In today's world that isn't much of a rebellion. But in 1960, on the campus of a Methodist college, in a state that only sold 3.2 beer, I felt it was a major rebellion. Some of the boys with whom I played bridge joined a private club like the Elks. In private clubs liquor was available. After classes, four of us would go to the club, order a Tom Collins and play bridge. We would have been expelled if the school authorities ever found out we were drinking. I was also under the legal age to drink. It was a risk legally and academically. I took the risk and I felt I was snubbing my nose at the rules and authority in general. Rules, it was believed by college students, were made to be broken. I rebelled and broke whatever rules I could at Wesleyan. Even my senior year, when I was so close to graduating, I took the chances and would stay out past 11pm. I had a friend put a wad of paper in the back door to keep it from locking and I would sneak back into the Dorm. My lights were off, my bed looked as if someone was sleeping in it when the RA (resident assistant) did her nightly room check. What was I doing out late at night? I was playing bridge, drinking a Tom Collins, and rejoicing in my freedom by wearing jeans. Shocking! If I had been caught I would have been expelled and all that work and all that money wasted. I wasn't caught. My rebellions are the only things I recall about Wesleyan with any joy.

I changed my major from Christian Education to Biology in the second semester of my freshman year. I was 19 and defiant. I didn't like the CE program. I thought the curriculum was elementary and an insult to my intelligence. Am I puffed up with self importance to say this? Perhaps. But I found a wonderful intellectual challenge in the Biology Department. I had taken advanced biology courses in High School. When it was time to sign up for a science course in my freshman year, I remember Dr. George Rossbach telling the parents and students at freshman orientation that his class was hard. He said something like, "Look at the student to your right and the student to your left—one of them won't be there next semester." I looked around and thought, "I'll be around and I'll pass." I was determined and I did. I remember saying to the CE professor once, "Well, Dr. Rossbach said such and such" in regards to some religious issue or question I might have had, to which she replied, "You can't take anything Dr. Rossbach has to say seriously on the matter because, after all, he's a Unitarian." I hated the narrow mindedness of the Christian education professor, as well as the theology that I was being taught. In biology no one seemed to care that I was a girl, so long as I did the work. I am grateful to this day that I changed majors. I enjoyed knowing Dr. Rossbach and I enjoyed studying under him. Under his tutelage I flourished in physiology, microbiology, comparative anatomy, botany, pathology, ecology and evolution. He hired me to be a lab assistant in my senior year for advanced physiology. By the time I graduated I had been inducted into the biology honor society, *Beta, Beta, Beta.* I tease and say I majored in the 3 Bs: Biology, Bridge and Booze, not necessarily in that order.

My first job after college was teaching biology and general science at the Thomas School for Girls in Rowayton, CT. Those first years of teaching were very much influenced by Dr. George Rossbach and the other professors in the science department at Wesleyan. For them and to them I continue to give thanks.

I had a second major in Sociology with Dr. Florence Schaffer. She was a delightful teacher, and one of her favorite quips had to do with mankind's ability to form society because of our "opposable thumbs." She was not on the CE's professor's most favorite list either. It became apparent that if I were to stay at Wesleyan and find any academic happiness, I needed to switch my major. And by doing so, I also switched my loyalty, my philosophy and views on life from the sacred to the secular. I left the church when I left the CE department. I did not return to the church for nearly 20 years. And that is another story.

I was on the Debate Team at college for two years. I had a "debate" scholarship and that was one reason why I felt compelled to stay when I knew that I was unhappy at Wesleyan. Our team was made up of two affirmative and two negative speakers. We traveled to the University of Pittsburgh for the North East regional debates. In 1960-1961 the debate topic for which all teams prepared was this: "That affordable health insurance should be every citizen's right". (or something like it . . . mandatory health insurance was the bottom line.) Here we are 50 years later and the topical subject is still paramount in social and political circles. At the Regional Level our team debated the teams of Harvard, Princeton, Yale, Dartmouth, and other notable colleges. Our school did not take the first place with the appropriate trophy but we beat some of the Ivy League schools and I recall we did place. We were very pleased with our performance.

We also traveled to Duke and to Winston-Salem College. When we were at Winston-Salem College, there was a sudden and severe snow storm which prevented us from getting back to Buckhannon dorm at the appointed time. Our Debate coach called the Dean of Women and told her of our dilemma, explaining that the town didn't have snow plows and we were stuck. She was not impressed with this explanation, and I don't think she believed the coach. When he told her that the only sign of snow removal were pick-up trucks pulling boards behind the truck beds, she relented and said we could stay one more day without penalty of being marked late or absent. The coach muttered something about if only his team were all males he wouldn't be in this position. Then he just smiled at me and said something like, "But I need you to secure the win as first affirmative speaker." We stayed another night at Winston-Salem College. Here we were, a team from Appalachia made up of four Caucasians at a

Black institution in a Jim Crow town. This was my first experience to see the signs, "For Whites Only." The signs, the segregated college system, the surprise snow fall, the lack of equipment and the Dean's begrudging attitude toward our coach's honesty helped to shape and reinforce my rebellions of rules and religion.

There are two other college incidents that are still ablaze in my memory. The first had to do with the Christmas Door decoration contest which I entered in my sophomore year. We were invited to decorate our doors for the Christmas season. I covered the entire door in black paper. Then I superimposed a Star of David in gold foil with gold streams of light coming from the star. In gold foil I cut out the letters to read: "Into a dark world came a Jew."

I was told to take my door decorations down. I refused and the RA tore it down in front of my eyes. I suppose if I had coined the pop expression "Jesus is the reason for the season" I may have won the contest. Yet, was not Jesus a Jew?

The second thing that happened in my sophomore year which helped to make my decision to do my junior year abroad in Mexico was this. Two girls, I knew one of them, were caught in bed together. I don't know if they were making love or not. But the RA thought they were and they were expelled. There was no "Gay& Straight Alliance" or PFLAG (Parents, Family and Friends of Lesbians and Gays) in 1962. No one dared admit they were homosexual. We were taught that all homosexuals were perverted, sick and deranged. There were no role models. Literature portrayed homosexuals as tormented souls. There was no one to talk to about sexual matters on campus for fear that if one confessed to homosexual feelings one would be reported and expelled. Wesleyan was not unusual for its day as a conservative Christian college.

My memories hold so few "good times" of college days. I do have some: Professors Rossbach, Shaffer and Jane Schanbel; Martha, Becky, Joyce, Bill, Bruce, bridge and the Elks, the beauty of autumn, the majestic hills, the play *Fantasticks,* summer vacations and finally graduation!

Arriving in Mexico City

In the fall of 1962 I said good-by to my weeping mother and father, boarded an airplane in Pittsburgh and headed for Newark, NJ to be met by Ed Mullen's family. The next day the two of us headed for Mexico City. Ed and I were the only West Virginia Wesleyan students doing our Junior-Year-Abroad study at the National University of Mexico in Mexico City.

Mother had made four new dresses for me. We had bought a shipping trunk and had it sent ahead to the address provided by Wesleyan. That address was the Mexican Methodist pastor/missionary who was responsible for making all arrangements for the American Students coming to study for the year. This was the first year that Wesleyan was using the Mexican program. I think it may have been the last year as well.

Let me say first that I did not speak Spanish. Ed was quite fluent, and I understand he has a PhD in languages and teaches Spanish at a university. I had taken three years of Spanish in High School and 2 sessions of college Spanish. I was able to read Spanish and understand what I read to some extent and I hoped that my Spanish would improve once I was immersed in the culture. Once I arrived in Mexico, I found myself so incredibly shy and afraid of making mistakes that I rarely spoke and I became overly dependent on my American roommate, Kathy, whom I met at the University on the first day of classes.

When Ed and I arrived in Mexico City's airport, the Mexican Reverend was there to meet us. He took us to his modest home and fed us, then announced that he would take Ed to his Mexican home where he was to live for the year. We arrived at a typical well-to-do neighborhood where every home was surrounded by a wall. The tops of the walls were covered in barbed wire or with broken glass shards embedded in the cement. Once the gates were opened and we drove into the courtyard, we were met by a lovely woman and her family. The house was made of a stucco material, painted yellow and the foyer of the home was done in beautiful ceramic tiles. Think of some of the Latin American movie sets and that is what Ed's adopted Mexican Home was like. He was being adopted by a family consisting of a mother, father, and several brothers. Ed and I made plans that the Reverend would pick us up the next day so we could register for classes at the University.

Having seen where Ed was living I felt more at ease as to where I might be living. When the Reverend and I got back into his beat-up car he said, "Your arrangements are still up in the air. So until I can come up with something, and my wife and I do not have room for you, I've made arrangements for you to stay at the local nunnery." He didn't call it a nunnery, he gave its name and it was a monastery for nuns.

It, too, had the high gated walls topped with bottle shards. It was not painted yellow. There were no beautiful ceramic floors. We were not met by a lovely family. We rang the bell at the oppressive massive oak door and waited until we were met by a very formidable nun in full habit. She immediately sent Reverend away and escorted me into the building. She gave me three keys: one for the outside gate, one for the front door and one for my room. I gathered enough from her that it would not be safe to leave. She took me to my room which consisted of a bed, a small table, and hooks for clothes. The bathroom was down the hall. Then she walked out of the room shutting the door behind her and there I stood in the middle of a bare room, without anything to remind me of home. My trunk had not arrived. I had a little suitcase which held a few extras. There were bars on my windows, as there are bars on most windows of Mexican homes, but I wasn't used to bars on the windows I can tell you. No phone. No way to let my parents know that I had arrived. No way to tell them I wanted to come home: NOW!

I sat on the bed for awhile and then decided as it grew dark that I should get ready for bed and that in the morning when I went to the University I would see Ed and surely the Reverend would have made other arrangements for me.

During the night I was awakened with the scurry of feet. When I turned on the lights I caught just a glimpse of those feet . . . they belong to rats. Not mice. Rats. God I was homesick and scared. When I met Reverend and Ed the next morning they were dismayed at my appearance:

my eyes were swollen shut, my arms looked as if I was clawed and I was an emotional wreck. They wanted to know what had happened to me. It was the mosquitoes. After dark they had descended upon me and I was allergic to mosquitoes. I took pills (pyrobenzamine) to combat swelling from mosquitoes. Where were the pills? In the trunk. I had all of my belongings with me and I told the Reverend under no circumstances was I going back to the nunnery; he would have to make other arrangements that day!

Once we got to the University we were overwhelmed with the size and beauty of the buildings. The major building was done in mosaics with colorful stories from Mexico's history. They had finished this area of the campus around 1954. Many famous artists were used for this project of updating the university's campus. It seemed enormous to us, coming from a small liberal arts college in the hills of West Virginia. Even today the school is generally considered to be the largest university in Latin America in terms of student population, campus and amenities.

At the registration office Ed had no trouble signing up for the courses he wanted. I was limited to those courses being taught in English. So I signed up for Mexican history and culture, the History of Mexican Art and Spanish. The person helping with the registrations was an American gal from Southern California. She was very helpful to me and inquired about my face. I told her of my awful night at the nunnery and I needing a place to stay. God provides! She said she was looking for a roommate. She said the apartment was on the bus route and it would only take 20 minutes to get to the university. If I would like, we could go meet the landlady after she was finished with her work. I said I would very much like to meet the landlady.

We went that very afternoon during siesta time, the first two hours of the afternoon when everything is so hot, and most work stopped. The Reverend went with us. We went to a very modest apartment building. The apartment had a living room, a dining room with a bar with bottles of alcohol in full view, two bedrooms and a bath. No kitchen. The cooking was done by a maid who lived in a room on the roof and who did the cooking on an open grill on the roof. There was no refrigeration. Shopping was done every day for the daily meals. The landlady was single and she had a small daughter, as did the maid. The landlady was a dancer.

She was part of the ensemble for the Ballet Folklórico de México de Amalia Hernández. This group was begun by Hernandez in 1952 and the troupe grew to 50 dancers by the time I came to Mexico. Many of the ensemble's works reflected the traditions of the indigenous cultures, and the costumes were elaborate and very beautiful. I was able to see several productions. I was enthralled by those performances and thrilled we were invited back stage to meet some of the dancers.

Well, the good Reverend said absolutely not. I could not stay there because she was a dancer and you know what that means. I said, I had no idea what that means. "Well," he said, "she will be exposing you to an environment that is not up to the Methodist standards: there will be dancing, drinking, smoking and God forbid, you will be exposed to homosexuals." I said I didn't give a tinker's damn about those things, I was not staying with those nuns another night. I told him when my trunk arrived please bring it to this address. And that was how I ended up living for a few months with a dancer from the Ballet Folklorico of Mexico. And that is how my relationship with the Reverend ended as he said he could no longer take responsibility for me. I didn't care. His looking after me had not done me any good.

Kathy and I shared a bedroom, we caught the bus down the street from the apartment to go to University and we did get to meet some of the other members of the Ballet group. It was a very nice apartment, and we were both sad when we had to leave and find other accommodations. My memory is very vague as to when and why we moved to another apartment which was far less exotic than the dancer's. The second apartment was smaller. The landlady and her brother shared the apartment: three bedrooms, and one large room. Again, the maid did all the work. She did the shopping and the cooking, the cooking being done outside, this time in a lot next to the apartment building. It was a good place and we were treated like family. We had a Mexican mother to hover over us and a Mexican Uncle/brother to protect our honor. That will be another story.

Defending My Honor

At the age of 20 I found myself in Mexico City for my "Junior Year Abroad" college program, totally naïve about almost everything. I had never seen people sleeping in hallways or on the sidewalk before. I led a sheltered life. I thought the maid who lived on the roof was most unfortunate, and I felt sorry for her. Never mind that she and her child had a roof over their heads, employment and plenty of food to keep her and her child healthy. I thought that she was most "unfortunate" because she had to be a maid and she was also the mistress of a wealthy married man. What did I know about living conditions in another part of the world, remote from Buckhannon, West Virginia or Pittsburgh, Pennsylvania? I had grown up in a Christian, middle class, American bubble. I knew nothing of the ways of the world, or of the ways of men and women in a third world class of society.

My one and only date at West Virginia Wesleyan was early during my freshman year. It was a "blind date" set up by a sophomore down the hall in my dorm. I don't remember his name. I remember I wore my prom dress which mother had made for my senior prom in High School. You will recall the dress was blue and it needed two crinolines to puff out the skirt. I liked the dress enough to bring it with me to college and it was the only "formal" dress I owned to go to this "formal" occasion on campus. The fellow, "my date" met me in the receiving hall of the dorm, and we went to the campus gymnasium where the dance was held. I don't remember exactly, but I suppose we timidly introduced ourselves. Once we got to the dance, he said he was going to go and get us some punch and so I waited for a half hour for him to return and then realized that he had other things to do. That was my introduction to college social life. I walked myself back to the dorm, took off my prom dress and it was never worn again. The epilogue to that story is that I never went to another dance at Wesleyan, not even to the Senior Formal.

So when I was asked to go to a dance at the YMCA in Mexico City, I wasn't too sure I wanted to go, but my roommate, Kathy, wanted to go. So we went. The dance was a celebration for the holiday, *Dia de los Muertos*, The Day of The Dead. The Mexicans celebrate this holiday for three days, from October 31-November 2. Candy sugar skulls are sold from various venues. Your name can be written in colored icing on the skull. Like our celebrations of Halloween here in the States, in Mexico there are lots of skeletons and coffins used as decorations in the homes and shops. On All Saints Day, November 1st, everyone goes to Mass and no one has to go to work. On All Souls Day, November 2nd, everyone visits the cemeteries where their beloveds are buried. People sometimes bring a picnic lunch and sit by the graveside with their families. They often leave fruit on the gravesite. If you think Halloween is a big celebration here in the States, you haven't seen anything until you have seen the celebrations of *Dia de los Muertos* in Mexico City as I saw it in 1962.

I want to digress for a moment, and tell you a story about how I tried to introduce the idea of *Dia de los Muertos* at the Greenville Baptist Church. Mexico was the country that the GBC's Women's Ministry was studying that year for their mission work. So I thought that as a church congregation we might learn about the Mexican holiday that corresponds to our Halloween. I thought I had presented the idea of how we could celebrate *Dia de los Muertos* to the deacons and they agreed on the ideas I presented. I suggested that we would initially gather for a simple lunch after worship, and I would encourage everyone to bring a photo and a small memento of a beloved who had died and that the table conversation would be that each person would share with the group, what the chosen memento meant to them and follow that up with stories about their beloved. I also told the deacons that I would explain the theology behind the Mexican *Dia de los Muertos* and how the holiday was a day of nostalgic remembrance, honor, and tribute to the deceased family members. All went well with the Deacons.

One woman of the congregation decided that after her "research" it was her learned opinion that we were asking the congregation to be involved with heathen practices and superstitious demon and spirits worship. She wrote to the Deacons and asked them to cancel the luncheon and our interpretation of remembering the dead. She began a phone campaign to stop the program as planned. She circulated printed material she had downloaded from the internet. It was grossly misleading and inaccurate, as well as biased, as to the true meanings of *Dia de los Muertos.* The deacons were unsettled but, to their credit, they did not tell me to "abort" the activities planned.

When the day arrived that we had set aside for our celebrations only 8 people showed up for lunch. (We had enough food and had planned on 100 people.) Those eight each brought a photo and memento, and we shared stories about our loved ones who had died, and we had plenty of food! The woman had caused such doubt within and among the members of the Board of Deacons and the congregation that the congregation boycotted the celebrations. It was a painful lesson for me to learn that people fear what they don't understand and that I must not have done a good enough job of educating the congregation on a cultural phenomenon that no one, except me, had ever experienced.

At the Day of the Dead dance I met Humberto in 1962. He was tall, dark and handsome, with gorgeous brown eyes and dark brown hair. He had a pencil thin mustache. He reminded me of Clark Gable! He was older than I was and he was employed as an engineer. He asked me to dance and we had quite a nice time. The next day he invited me to join him for lunch after he went to Mass. He bought me a sugar skull and had my name written on it. We went to the cemetery where his parents were buried. We spent time with each other when I wasn't in class.

He took me to some of the famous sites in Mexico City. We went to the National Museum of Anthropology in Mexico City in Chapultepec Park. The park is much larger than Roger Williams Park in Providence, RI. But the parks are similar because of the vast areas for people to gather and picnic, to stroll along the walkways and visit the shops. We spent considerable time in the Museum of Anthropology. I have a vivid memory of seeing the Aztec Sun Stone which we had been introduced to in elementary school as the "Aztec Calendar."

I learned from Humberto that the stone was not a calendar at all, but a monument/story about the Aztec Nation, its rise and its fall. It is at least 12 feet in diameter with intricate carvings and symbols. It is a very important artifact for all Mexicans and I was privileged to see it . . . even if I did not understand it. The National Cathedral was also a wonderful visit. Next to the Cathedral is a smaller, quainter chapel where people come to pray for healings. There are little metal replicas of legs, arms, torsos and heads left behind on the walls of the chapel. These totems represent the "answered" prayers of people who needed healing for their leg or arm or hand, etc. We saw this same phenomena in some of the Greek Orthodox churches on my trip to Greece and Turkey "following the footsteps of Paul" in 2007.

Humberto and I were not a couple. We probably held hands and gave the appearance of a dating couple, but there was nothing more to our platonic friendship. He was a nice man who showed me some of the sites of Mexico City and he was an attentive companion. My Mexican "foster" mother and Mexican "foster" uncle asked me questions about him, many of which I had no answer: e.g., where did he live? where did he work,? who were his parents? what were his intentions? I could not answer their questions. Since I was living in their house I was now their responsibility and they "hovered" like hens to a chick. In 1962 "good" Mexican women were not permitted to date without a chaperone. My Mexican family didn't want me to see Humberto because it just was not the way things should be in their culture. Wives and sisters including "foster children" were to be protected.

On the other hand, "Gringas" (feminine for Gringo) like Kathy and me seemed to be fair game on the buses, in the elevators and on the streets. Men would try and grab me in the elevators, they would shout, (what I assumed were profanities), at me when walking down the street, and men would rub up against me if I had an outside seat on the bus. I very much disliked this public humiliation. One day on the bus a man was trying to sexually assault me. I had just come from the open-air market. I had bought a wooden beater used for making hot chocolate and while this man was trying to grope me I hit him on the head with the beater. I now know it was a foolish move on my part, because I could have been hurt. The man behind my seat saw what had been transpiring. He stood up and grabbed the man and the two of them wrestled themselves off the bus. My honor was being protected by a stranger. Kathy and I decided we would take taxis more often.

One night as Humberto and I sat in his car (I'm not sure if it was his car or a borrowed car) in front of my Mexican home, and he tried to kiss me. It was the first time since we started our friendship. I wasn't experienced at kissing and I am sure I was quite awkward. But I didn't say no and I found that kissing was quite pleasant. It was night and I knew I was expected home, but lingering in front of the house kissing had more appeal than being in on time. Suddenly, his passions began to get out of hand. I was scared. All I wanted to do was get out of the car. He started to cry and he apologized and he tried to calm me. I just wanted out of the car. Finally, I got myself into the house, shaking and I went immediately to my room. My "mother" and "uncle" wanted to know what the matter was. I simply could not tell them. I didn't hear from Humberto for weeks.

Kathy didn't understand why I was so upset.

At some later point in time, she introduced me to a man by the name of Jorge. Jorge took me to a night club that had an "Arabian Night" theme. There were private booths along the wall, with curtains for privacy. I managed to get out of that situation with dignity and virtue intact and when I got home I told Kathy about the adventure. In the morning she told "Uncle" at the breakfast table. He jumped up from the table, went into his bedroom and came out carrying a pistol. I asked where he was going with a pistol and I was informed he was going after Jorge to defend my honor and his. After that I didn't go out on a date without Kathy.

Humberto kept in touch. He even wrote to me when I returned home to Pennsylvania. He said he wanted to marry me and that he would come and live in the USA. There was no love interest for me as far as Humberto was concerned, and my parents were relieved. What on earth would they do with a Mexican son-in-law? Did he love me? Maybe! Was I a way for him to come to the states? Maybe! Did I love him? Not enough to marry him. But he was the first man I had ever kissed and I enjoyed it. I don't suppose anyone ever forgets her first kiss.

Camp Mogisca
Sparta, NJ
1960-1964

What kept me going during my college years? Camp Mogisca! Where did I find fulfillment, encouragement, happiness and friendships? Camp Mogisca!

Camp Mogisca was the Morris Area Girl Scout Camp. The camp was located on a large lake in Sparta, NJ. I arrived in June of 1960 following my graduation from High School. My folks were hesitant to let me go so far from home for my first real summer job. They drove me to camp and where we met Phyllis Douglas, the camp director. My folks checked out the living environment, met some of the other staff, talked to the returning counselors and left me there on my own. I was a raw recruit. I knew nothing about camping, really. I had slept in a tent once in the back yard. I had been a Girl Scout but only up to junior high school. When it was decided that I could go to Camp Mogisca, my Dad insisted that since I was going to be responsible for some young campers that I should take a life saving course before going to camp. I accomplished this at the Jewish Recreation Center in Pittsburgh, Pennsylvania. I'm not one who is very fond of swimming but it was a very good idea to have the Red Cross Life Saving Course certificate. Also at Dad's insistence, I took a CPR and a First Aid course.

My first summer at Camp Mogisca was exhilarating. I was assigned to the Pioneer Unit, the unit for 7th and 8th grade girls. We lived in tents across the lake from the main dining hall and administration buildings. Our tents were nestled among the trees, birches and oaks, maples and ash and we fell asleep to the lapping of the water against the rocks and shore. Each bed had a mattress and two "T" shaped poles which we had to lash to the bed frame. The first thing I had to learn was "how to lash." Dad helped and mother and I maneuvered the mosquito netting we had brought, up and over the "T" poles and we created a protected little cocoon for me. I was very allergic to mosquitoes and here I was living by a lake in mosquito paradise. Fortunately for me, I was able to have my little aqua blue/green pills of pyribenzamine, a prescription antihistamine, which kept me from itching or swelling from the mosquitoes. The side effect was that I had dry mouth all summer . . . but I didn't itch.

Camp Mogisca had a unit for Brownies, the youngest girls, and a unit for the Senior Scouts. Thus, the age range of girls at camp went from elementary to high school. The youngest girls ate most of their meals in the dining hall and everyone ate their noon meal in the dining hall. After the noon meal there was group singing. The Assistant Director led the singing in the summer of 1960. She did not have the talent for this task, but apparently it was part of her job description. One day I was complaining about the singing and the poor job she was doing while I was in the community bath facilities in main camp, and the camp director over-heard my complaints. She called me into her office and gave me a mild enough tongue lashing for not being supportive of a fellow staff member and then she said, "But I do have to agree with you. She is dreadful. I've heard you sing. Do you think you could lead the singing?" Me? I sang in the school choirs, but I had never led singing. "Yes," I said. "I think I can at least give it a try." And that was the beginning of five summers of being the camp's song leader. I just loved it. With my gift of gab and making fun of myself, I was able to get the girls and the staff to truly enjoy the typical camp songs of the day. During my last year as camp song director in 1964, we made a recording. The songs were simple and catchy. Some songs called for harmony and we sang them quite lovely. Other songs were boisterous and we had to shout, jump up, turn around, sit down and clap. The girls loved the singing. We would sing around the campfire at night. We would sing when we spent the night tending to the kiln which fired the pottery projects. We would sing on the way to the dining hall and back to the units. We sang on our canoe trips going down the river from Dingsman's Ferry to the Delaware Water Gap. We never needed a reason to make music. We sang all the time and I was as happy as I could be. Yes, I enjoyed gathering the girls together at noontime to sing. I enjoyed the jokes I told them, the silly stories, the running commentary I would give of what was happening that day.

My second year of camp staff, I returned as Program Director and Camp Song Director. I was no longer in a unit, but rather I was planning the themes for the summer; the all camp gatherings, the parties and activities. But the best part of the day was the noontime singing. I introduced the idea of special hats for special occasions. I remember my mother and I shopping for those hats together and thinking of fun ways to introduce the idea of "The Birthday" hat, "The Leader's" hat, "The Good Deed" hat, "The Director's" hat and "The Skunk" hat. The latter was a gag hat for someone who did something silly or very funny or maybe even rather stupid . . . and the girls just loved it, especially when a favorite counselor was asked to wear the "Skunk" hat.

Each year during the long and lonely days at college, I would dream of being at camp with Phyllis Douglas, Betty Lee Watson and the other women I loved. I thought about programs, songs, and trips the campers could take. I investigated how to teach the staff various skills they would need for their units. Since I was part of the camp administration, I was always part of the staff training week and mid-season staff development trainings. Every vacation I had at college, I spent in Morristown, NJ with Phyllis Douglas making plans for the summer.

My final year at Camp was in 1964 and I was the Assistant Camp Director under Betty Lee Watson, as the Camp Director. Those summers were the best summers of my life. The summers were purpose driven and rewarding. I was able to hone my skills in leadership development. Phyllis Douglas was my mentor. I watched her lead and I learned from her. She was the most important person in my life during those very formative years. She lead from conviction and passion and taught me when I had to be strong and tough and when a gentle hand was needed. Dr. Rossbach taught me the material I needed for my field of biology, but it was Phyllis Douglas who taught me how to be a teacher, and a leader. She saw in me strengths I didn't know I had. She cultivated my skills and believed in me. She was the one who really and sincerely listened. She was the one who advised. She was the older woman that I think every girl needs, (aside from one's mother and other kin); someone who shows unconditional love and at the same time knows when to be as tough as nails. I can think of no other woman who helped to mold me, love me, scold me, encouraged me, and taught me what it means to be a woman and a leader, than Phyllis Douglas. She gave me courage and confidence. She helped to build my character so that I could help to make the world a better place. She certainly made ***MY*** world a better place. I loved her. And I loved my years at Camp Mogisca on a lake in Sparta, NJ.

Why Mothers Get Gray Hair

When my mother died she had beautiful white hair. As a little girl I would sit on her bed and watch while she combed her hair before dinner. Every day my mother would set some time aside for herself when she got ready for Daddy to come home. She would put on a pretty dress, do her make-up and fuss with her hair. Her hair was brown then. And I would watch her get ready and think she was the most beautiful woman I had ever seen. I think it is a nice way for a child to see her mother, even if not realistic. I mean mother was not Marilyn Monroe or Loretta Young but I thought she was lovely. Daddy did too!

She was, as Dad said, "a looker." She had beautiful legs which Dad was always ready to point out. I recall every night as we were growing up, she would come around to his end of the dinner table and pour him his tea, and he would gently slide his hand up her skirt and pinch her. Then she would say, "Oh Edward!" I'm sure she loved it. My brother, Ted, has inherited mother's gorgeous white hair. Mother had a small button nose, slightly turned up, and I have her nose. She was of average height, thin, and she had style.

I remember once when my daughter, Rebecca, was small and I was getting dressed, she stared at me with her big blue eyes and said something to the effect, "When I grow up will I be fancy like you?" I don't believe she meant the clothes I was going to wear, but rather how "fancy" a woman is, as distinguished from a girl. In my adult household it was I who marveled at the indescribable beauty that my daughter had grown into during her adolescence and especially by the time she had entered High School.

My mother had good reason for her hair turning white, although it did not happen overnight, as some stories go. On the last day of school in my first grade year, I was allowed to wear the dress I had worn as flower girl for my Aunt Joanne's wedding the summer before. Mother had made the dress, blue organza with hand embroidered daisies worn over a blue taffeta slip. In the wedding pictures I am seen with Shirley Temple like curls in my "wedding dress" wearing my black patent leather "Mary Janes," and I was far more interested in the rice on the church steps than posing for the wedding photo. In any case, my Aunt Joanne's wedding was an occasion for my mother to make me this very special dress, so wearing it to school was very special and quite exciting.

We had to walk to school in those days (Oh no, not the, "in my day we walked three miles to school, in the snow, and uphill both ways" bit.) Yes, we did walk, but I have no idea how far it was. I would guess today it would not be over one mile. We had to walk over a street car bridge which was made of wood. On the walkway there were often places where the boards where missing and the big boys would tease the little girls that they would fall through or they would pick us up and threaten to throw us over. My walks to school when I was in first grade were a scary thing.

One day, when I was in the third grade and tall enough so that I could see over the railing of the bridge and not worry about the missing boards, I saw a man lying next to the footings of the bridge. He had no head. That was my first, but not last, time of seeing the remains of someone who had jumped from the bridge. My mother never liked the idea that I had to walk to school. We had no car so she couldn't drive me, and at that time there were no school busses. By the time I was in fifth grade, I was given street car passes. I don't know if my mother helped get that "benefit" through the school board, but I do know she was very pleased. That street car bridge caused my mother to get lots of gray hairs.

On the last day of First Grade, as I was walking in the alley behind the houses on Renton Avenue wearing my very special dress, I was not thinking about anything special and I was not really paying attention. Directly behind our house and across the alley lived our neighbors, the Schnoffers. They had a white pit bull-type dog. I am really not sure the exact breed, but I do remember that every child in the neighborhood was warned not to get too close to that dog. He was chained to a dog house which was located right beside the alley. The chain was long enough for the dog to get half way across the alley. Since I was not paying attention, I didn't realize that I was on the wrong side of the alley . . . the side with the dog, the dog which everyone was afraid of, especially me. Suddenly, my lunch box was thrown in the air as the dog attacked me, and I was dragged into his dog house. He was trying to make a meal of me. I was only 6 years old at the time, and I was wearing my best and very special dress. It was a nightmare. I screamed and cried, kicked and somehow managed to get away from the dog, and I dashed up the terraces to the house screaming for mother. My dress was thrown off. I was running in just my slip which was covered in blood and ripped in several places. I could barely see with all the blood running down my face.

That is all that I can remember. How did mother get me to the doctor's without a car? I have no memory. I had twenty some stitches in my face and under my chin, the dog's eyetooth went through my nose and over my left temple. The dog made a gash so severe that the doctor told my mother (and she told me) that a fraction deeper or closer to the temple and I would have bled to death. Who came and watched the kids while I was taken to the doctor's? I have no memory. My brother Ted was four and my sister Nancy was one. Those days were not as litigious as the days we live in now. My parents did not sue or even ask for help with the medical bills. And none was offered. My Dad spoke to the neighbors and said they would have to get rid of the dog, but not before it could be tested for rabies. As the story goes, the Schnoffers sent the dog to their parents' farm and it got away and was run over by a train. That meant that there were no rabies tests, and I had to suffer through the routine of rabies shots in my belly. Again, I've blocked out of my memory of those shots but I am sure my mother never blocked out any of it . . . reason enough for more gray hairs.

Speaking of rabies shots, on Mother's Day of 2008 my youngest grandson, Isaac, was scratched by a woodchuck (also known as a groundhog) in his back yard. This woodchuck was acting very peculiar and charged several adults who had come to Isaac's aid. There has never been any proof that the woodchuck was rabid because the Department of Environmental Management (DEM) never really looked for it, nor did they tell the neighbors to be careful. Weeks later when a horse was diagnosed with rabies the DEM and the police began to warn the neighbors about the possibility of rabies in the area.

At that very moment when Isaac encountered the woodchuck, I was having dinner with my daughter when suddenly she received a phone call that Isaac was being rushed to the emergency care clinic in Greenville, and she was to meet the boy and his father there. At the clinic they said Isaac must go to Hasbro Children's Hospital where the staff decided to start him on the rabies vaccine which is now given in the leg. It is still a painful procedure and there are several weeks of these shots. I hope that Isaac will be able to block out this event much as I have blocked out mine. My daughter is starting her own set of gray hairs.

The colossal accident that my mother had to handle, and which certainly qualifies for many gray hairs, was the time my brother's leg was burned. Ted and I were near the burning trash barrel which was located on the lower terrace of the property. A neighbor child came over to play, and the three of us would put our sticks into the burn barrel and get them to flame and then we would write our names in smoke in the air. We did this for a long time . . . getting our sticks to catch fire, blowing out the flame and using the smoke to write in the sky. Ted was five years old and I was seven. We had been repeatedly told not to play near the burn barrel. Writing our names with smoke took precedence over obeying the rules.

The neighbor's flaming stick dropped onto Ted's pant leg and immediately his light weight cotton pants caught on fire. I ran as fast as I could yelling that "Teddy was on fire" and Teddy was running right behind me. Mother heard us and began running down from the top floor and managed to meet us in the cellar where she wrapped Ted in blankets and smothered the flame. Remember, Ted was only five years old with a tiny little leg and that little leg was now in big big trouble.

Similar to my dog bite story, I have no recollection of how mother got Ted to the doctor's or who stayed with Nancy and me. What I do remember is that my mother saved Ted's leg. The doctor told her Ted's leg was so severely burned from the knee to the ankle that they should amputate the leg. Apparently mother said that her father was an MD and that with his advice and her attention she would not give the doctors permission to amputate. She asked for and was given a chance to save it.

I can still recall what the house smelled like after the burn, a sweet/ pungent/decaying smell. Mother had to dress the leg several times a day. The neighbors came and helped to entertain Ted. He worked hard to learn to walk again and he was promised goodies as encouragements. He was able to walk by the time he started first grade. Over the years, Ted has had several skin grafts. During the Vietnam War era, the draft board doctor told Ted that his sisters would be drafted before he would be, a small consolation for a lifetime of being reminded every time he looks at his leg, what playing with fire can do. And whenever I see his leg, I am reminded that in our Brownie Scout meeting just a few days after the fire we learned what to do if anyone catches on fire . . . to drop and roll. I still regret that I didn't know that rule and instead ran as fast as I've ever run to get Mother, with Teddy following. It was our mother's heroic nursing and her stubborn nature which helped to save Ted's leg. What's a few more gray hairs? She earned them.

Helen A. Mellott 1940

My Dad
A Man for All Seasons

My Dad loved to tell jokes and stories. He had an infectious laugh. When my youngest sister, Martha, told him the story of her visit with the gynecologist, he could hardly control his tears. The story went something like this: the gynecologist was a young and handsome man. I was with her in the examining room, with my head and eyes politely turned away. When the doctor was finished with his examination he told Martha she could get dressed, and Martha said, "Doctor, does this mean we are going steady now?"

I think we all inherited Dad's love of a good story. Dad not only loved to tell stories and jokes, he also loved the theatrics of dressing up and being silly. When he and mother bought their place at America Outdoors in Fort Myers, Florida, he had plenty of opportunities to "show off", as mother would say. At the parties for Valentine's Day, St. Patty's Day, New Year's Eve, and Halloween, everyone could count on Ed to be part of the follies or entertainment of the evening. We have photos of Dad dressed as cupid and baby New Year's with about the same costume, consisting of just a sheet wrapped to look like a diaper. On one Halloween he painted his chest and belly to look like a face. He would do just about anything to get a laugh. And, oh how he loved to sing! He had an excellent voice and was a good singer; he sang bass in the Ingomar Methodist Church choir for many years.

Martha takes after him and does the same sort of thing when it comes to dressing up for different celebrations. She makes all her own costumes. One election year she was a "bleeding heart liberal." She took yards and yards of red rayon material and fashioned it into a heart and stuffed the heart with polyfoam. This contraption fit over her body with her head and arms sticking out of the enormous heart. A dagger was plunged into the heart with a red gel dripping from the stab wound, thus, a bleeding heart liberal. On other occasions she designed costumes and became a lounge lizard, a sick puppy, and an Egyptian queen. For the queen's costume she used a blue plastic shower curtain that had various motifs of suns, stars and moons on it. This shower curtain was draped over her in toga fashion and she wore a rhinestone tiara. She squeaked as she walked. When she was dressed as a sick puppy, she had a thermometer in her mouth and she went to the local veterinarian's office. She asked the receptionist if she could speak to the doctor. When he came out to see her, she took gummy worms out of her pocket, showed the veterinarian and asked if he had anything for a sick puppy. She didn't know this vet, but after this little visit they became good friends. She and Dad had no trouble letting down their hair . . . well, Dad in his later years didn't have much hair to let down.

Dad was easygoing, and fun to be around. He liked to swim and hike, and take the church youth groups white water rafting down the Youghiogheny River. During his last years, when his Parkinson's disease confined him to a wheel chair, Martha found ways to take him swimming.

Dad was diagnosed with Parkinson's disease in August 2001 following elective colon surgery. He never fully regained his health after that surgery, and the surgery exacerbated the Parkinson's disease which no one had suspected he had. The last 41 months of Ed's life were months of frustrations and confinement. He spent 3 years at the Passavant Health Center in Zelienople, PA. near his son, Ted's, home. In July of 2004 Ed moved to the Overlook Health Center in Pascaog, RI where his daughters Lynne and Martha were able to help care for him. He attended all our family functions and enjoyed being with his family, and especially his grandchildren and the great-grandsons. During all this time, Dad never once said, "Why me?" He remained hopeful, cheerful and outgoing. He made friends wherever he went throughout his life and, certainly, during those years of confinement he endeared himself to the staff. Some folk complain about everything. I never really heard my Dad complain about much. At least, that is how I remember him! I know he hated being in a nursing home. I know he hated that his body was not performing for him as it had all his life. I know he hated having his children lead him to the bathroom and help him with all daily functions, but he never complained.

He would give you his most charming smile and say something funny to lighten the tension. He died peacefully, May 4, 2005, in Pascoag, RI, at the age of 89. He had been determined to live to be 100 but it was not meant to be.

Dad loved women. He would point out women, young or older, who he thought were attractive. He loved Marian Benson's apple pie and this would infuriate mother when he would say, "Honey, this pie is wonderful, but not quite up to Marian's." Dad liked to have meat, potatoes and vegetables for dinner and, of course, a little dessert. There were very few casseroles that mother made that he would eat. Basically, Dad wanted a real dinner. Pasta was not considered a real dinner. Soups were adequate for lunch but not for dinner, and that included a hearty chili. Mother worked very hard to please him and always on a limited budget.

Dad went to college at Penn State, graduating in 1939 with a BS degree in metallurgy. Following his graduation he worked for Republic Steel Company in Youngstown, Ohio for four years. I was born in Youngstown on July 30, 1942. My dad joined the Navy in April, 1943. Mother tells me he just came home one day and announced he had enlisted because he didn't want to take the chance and be drafted. He served from April, 1943 through November, 1946 during WWII on the escort carrier, Kasaan Bay CVE69. For many years he served in the naval reserves. I remember one night when we were expecting him to come home from Reserves and the door opened, but instead of seeing Dad coming through the door, we saw a tiny copper colored Collie puppy. What a surprise! We named the dog Penny. (Copper . . . Penny—get it!). She was a wonderful dog and very beautiful. We had her for years. I had never seen my mother cry until the night when Penny lay in her lap, dying from some sort of poisoning. That is my first memory of losing a beloved pet and seeing my mother cry.

Dad and a few of his friends started Merit Machinery in 1955. Prior to 1955, he worked for the William K. Stamets Company. Sometimes, when I was going to go visit him at work, I was allowed to get the streetcar at the foot of the hill from Renton Ave and ride to downtown Pittsburgh. A few of those times I would take my brother, Ted. I didn't like taking Ted because he would embarrass me by hanging and swinging on the poles in the streetcar. (Some people would call a streetcar a trolley. Streetcars ran on tracks) When we went to see Dad at the Stamets Company, we would get off the streetcar in front of the Gimbels department store, cross the street and go into the Jenkins Arcade Building. It seemed like a huge building at the time. Maybe it was! There were other offices in the building and we would take the elevator up to the level where Dad's office was with its embossed frosted-glass window, *William K. Staments*. Staments made a great deal of money during the war selling fabricating and machine tool equipment. The country's need for this type of machinery lasted through most of the 1970s. Dad and his friends who formed Merit Machinery sold the same type of machine tool equipment but their offices and show rooms were not in downtown Pittsburgh but in the North Hills section of the city. By the 1970s Dad often talked about how the manufacturing companies of this country were losing ground to cheaper methods and cheaper machines from Germany, Japan and China. By the time Dad retired in 1994, Merit Machinery was a shell of its former robust years. Scholastic industrial arts programs helped to keep the company afloat. Yet, as children, we never knew Dad to worry about money or the business. If our Dad had these worries, we were shielded from such worries by him. Mother, on the other hand, kept us all on a short leash and ran a very tight household. As a child of the depression, my mother could squeeze a nickel until the buffalo yelled. Mother kept impeccable accounts of every penny she spent. I find that I still do that. Mother managed the household affairs. I find that I still do that. Mother knew how much she had to work with and she had a budget for her funds. She was not one to borrow money or spend money she didn't have. There would be no easy credit for my mother. I find I am the same way. I was not raised during the Great Depression, but the depression affected my mother's life style and pretty much established how my mother raised her children and ran her household.

Mother was a no nonsense parent. Today, the expression or buzz word is "Zero Tolerance." If there was a problem, like when I rolled the family Ford station wagon under a truck the first time I drove the car by myself, I called home and asked to speak to Dad. Mother had answered the phone. "I want to speak to Dad." "Why do you want to talk to him, what's the matter?" she said. "Nothing, I just need to talk to Dad." And this went on until she finally turned the phone over to Dad. Dad was the non-disciplinarian. Dad was approachable. Dad rarely raised his voice. I would not say my Dad was a softy, but he was so much easier to get along with than mother. I think we were all intimidated by mother. She had a sharp tongue, a mercurial temper, a strong sense of what was right and what was wrong and she was forever worried about what the neighbors would think.

My sisters and I have said to each other more than once, that we hoped to marry a man like our father. Not one of us did! We wanted someone with his sense of humor, his gentleness, his love of the out-of doors, his tender ways with his family, his outrageous ways when he flirted, his dependability and self control. The man we hoped for and thought we would marry would have his devotion to his country, his home and his church. We wanted, in our mates, someone who loved us as much as Dad loved our mother. We wanted someone who worked hard at his profession and loved being at his home. He was a Dad who enjoyed being home and he represented Home. He represented stability, love, humor, common sense and every good virtue known to man. He could fix anything and everything. What a shock to learn that not all men know how to fix everything. What a shock to learn that not all men are as dependable and trustworthy as our Dad. What a shock to find that not all men are gentle in speech or in actions. What a shock to discover that not all men like staying home with family, puttering in the yard, fixing something at the work bench, making a lamp or coffee table, helping with a craft or science fair project or being with the family in church on Sundays. No, not all men are like my Dad. He was very special. I am so glad he was my Dad and thankful for the gifts he gave to me.

Edward L. Caughey 1941

The Adventures and Shenanigans of My Grandfather's Skeleton

When my grandfather Mellott died, grandmother told me that I could have his skeleton. When I tell people this or say that about the skeleton, "Oh, it was my grandfather's," most people just look at me or they freak out. Then I laugh and say, "Not my grandfather's skeleton, skeleton, his medical specimen of a skeleton."

I've had more fun with that skeleton. When it was given to me, the bones were all connected by wire and the whole thing was neatly folded into a wooden box or crate. The skull's jaw was missing some wires on one side, so you could say it was slack jawed. My grandfather might have bought this skeleton while he was in medical school at Baltimore University, graduating in 1909. Baltimore University is now known as the University of Maryland Medical College. Grandfather did his residency at Maryland General Hospital at the age of 29. This particular skeleton was natural, i.e. of real bone. Today, most study skeletons are made of plastic. I have no idea as to the skeleton's value in 1964, when I received this remarkable gift. I did know it was a female skeleton by the width and depth of the pelvic bones. I never gave the skeleton a name, because it was too much fun to refer to it as, "My grandfather's skeleton."

My grandmother felt that I should have grandfather's skeleton because I had just finished college with a bachelor of science degree in biology and I was about to begin my first teaching position as a science teacher at the Thomas School for Girls in Rowayton, Connecticut.

I remember the day I picked up the crate of bones. Grandmother had stored the crate in the laundry room of their home at 600 Maplewood Ave in Ambridge, PA. The laundry room was downstairs, that is, on the basement level along with the dining room, kitchen, pantry and furnace room with its coal chute. In the laundry room there were two sinks, one was used for the first rinse and the second for the final discharge of laundry water from the washing machine at the end of the day. The washing machine had a big metal tub or drum into which the clothes were placed and the water came in to cover them. There was a hose to dump the water back out into the sink. Then the washed, but wet, clothes went through a spin cycle, and you took the spun wet clothes out of the tub and placed them carefully through the wringer which squeezed more water out of the clothes before they were hung on the outdoor line to dry. Also in the laundry room was a large clothes "mangle" which was an iron with rollers that pressed the enormous linen table clothes, sheets, pillow cases and other flat wear. Flat irons, with their removable handles were put on the stove top to heat up and were used on ironing boards for shirts, dresses, blouses and other clothes. A laundry woman came to the house once a week to do the laundry. Amid the various boxes and crates, laundry soaps, bottles, and sundry stuff stored on the shelves in this laundry room was the box of grandfather's skeleton stored there at least since 1954 when Albert Nebraska Mellott, MD died.

The first adventure that this skeleton had with me was our trip to Connecticut in the late summer of 1964. Although I swore I would never be a teacher like my mother, her sisters and her mother, the only job I could find in the field of biology was at the Thomas School for Girls in Rowayton, CT.—far from home in more ways than miles! I loaded my nine year old 1955 green Studebaker, which looked like an upside down bathtub, with all of my earthly possessions—which really weren't all that much; some college room embellishments, a suitcase of clothes and my books. And of course, I had the skeleton. What a wonderful teaching prop for senior high biology and advanced biology students! I took the skeleton out of its crate, checked for any damage and decreed it was perfect. It rode in the front seat with me sitting upright, just like an anorexic passenger.

Off we went from Peebles Road, Pittsburgh to Rowayton, Connecticut in my little green Studebaker, loaded to the gills and my grandfather's skeleton setting upright next to me on the passenger side. There were no seat belts in my car, so when I had to make a stop I would throw my right arm over across the bony chest and keep the skeleton from flipping onto the floor. I balanced her right hand up against the window and put a cigarette between her bony phalanges. What a sight we made! Whenever we stopped for food or gas we caused quit a stir. Sometimes people would ask about it and sometimes people would say incredulously, "Did you know you have a skeleton in there?" DUH . . . But I would smile sweetly at their disbelief and say, "Yes, I know. It's my grandfather's skeleton," and then drive off. Once, just outside of Greenwich, Connecticut on route 95N I stopped at the Howard Johnson and bought two ice cream cones. When I returned to the car, as usual, there was a crowd staring through the passenger side window, and I smiled, unlocked my door, got in and put one ice cream cone in the hands of the skeleton and drove off. I can still see the crowd shaking their heads and murmuring, "Did you see that?!"

I took the skeleton to Pine Point School in Stonington, Connecticut where I taught the first time from 1966-1971. I had been hired by Alan Houghton to be the department chair for this independent school of Kindergarten through ninth grade. I taught sixth, seventh and ninth grade students and one year I had the third graders once a week. The skeleton never went to meet the third graders but the other science classes were quite familiar with my grandfather's skeleton. When I finally retired from teaching and tutoring at Pine Point I gave the skeleton to the school. The last time I returned to the school, the skeleton was hanging in the new Mitchell Building, but the skull was missing. Some prankster, perhaps at Halloween, took it, and I felt quite badly grandfather's skeleton was no longer whole.

Before I had given it away, I used to have the skeleton meet and greet trick or treaters at Halloween in our home in Misquamicut, Rhode Island where the kids came into the house, and the bowl of candy was in the skeleton's lap. I had the skeleton sit in front of the picture windows at our A-frame house on Greenhaven Road, Pawcatuck, Connecticut to greet the kids on Halloween night. But there has never been more fun with the skeleton than driving from Pennsylvania to Connecticut in the late summer of 1964 with a cigarette in its hand and an ice cream cone in the other, in that ugly 1955 green Studebaker. How I wish I had them both back.

The Great Northeast Blackout

My scientific training was limited to the biology courses offered at West Virginia Wesleyan College. I had one summer of internship at the New England Institute for Medical Research in Ridgefield, Connecticut where I spent time in the genetic and the physics departments.

After that summer internship I realized I knew very little about physics and so I decided to apply for a National Science Foundation grant to study the subject of physics while I was teaching at the Thomas School for Girls in Rowayton, Connecticut. The year was 1965. I was, indeed, awarded a grant, and it came with a list of schools where I could study physics using this very generous grant. I was thrilled! I looked over the catalog of schools, not knowing anything about any of them. I was a homespun gal from Pittsburgh, and I was not knowledgeable about schools in the Northeast. Since I could drive to New York City in just one hour, I selected a school in the city. I applied for admission for one physics course at Yeshiva University. I had read the ratings and some reviews of its Physics department and was convinced that it was a good choice. The day I was to start classes I left the Thomas School in Rowayton, and took route 95 south to the Major Deegan Expressway toward Amsterdam Ave. in the Bronx. Just being in that location, I anxiously started looking for Yeshiva University. The biggest city I had ever driven in was Pittsburgh. Once I got into the area of Amsterdam and 175th Street I was lost. I parked my car, put the money in the meter and headed across the street where several men were talking. "Excuse me," I said to the men who were all dressed in black and had very long beards. "Could you . . . ." And before I could ask for directions these men spun on their heels, did a 180 degree turn and hurried off. "How rude," I thought. Well, I would find someone else and ask for directions. The next set of men, dressed in the same manner gave me the same treatment. I was very perplexed and now quite anxious to find the University in order to register. After many attempts to get directions, I went into a deli shop, and the person there gave me directions. It turned out I was not too far away from my destination, so I could leave my car and walk. After I had registered, I found my classroom and discovered that my professor was from Russia and his accent made it difficult for me to understand him. I was the only woman in the class. My lab partners shunned and abandoned me—you'd have thought that I was a leper. I was on my own!

Within a few weeks of struggling through this class, I realized that I was also the only Gentile! What did this "SHIKSA" know about Judaism? Not a thing! I learned that the Hasidic Jews I had asked for directions did not speak to women on the streets, Jew or Gentile. What did I know? The entire experience of trying to study physics, as a gentile woman, in a Jewish University, with a professor I could not understand and no classmates to seek their help was all very frustrating. I wanted to quit more than once, yet I had received this grant and I was feeling obligated. But I really did want to quit!

Then, one day, in the evening of November 9, of 1965, when I arrived at the University, I found that the street lights, the buildings, everything was dark except for the light provided by the headlights of the cars on the street. Strange! I knew that lights ought to be on, but there were none. It was nighttime, and even the traffic lights were not working. Several men were directing traffic and they were not wearing uniforms, so I'm sure they were volunteers. I asked around if anyone knew what was going on. I was told that all classes had been canceled. The power was off; the city was in total darkness. I just turned around and headed back to Rowayton, totally in the dark, literally and figuratively. I took this blackout as a symbolic and prophetic sign that I was already enough in the dark and out of my element and that I did not have to finish the course. Enough was enough! I came to the conclusion that regarding the night of the 1965 Great Blackout I will always remember where I was and what I was doing and that I acknowledged this event as a "Heavenly" sign telling me that it was OK to quit on physics.[2] I found my way home to the Thomas School and bunked in with another teacher who had a fireplace in her home. Her friendship, her years of experience as a teacher and the warmth of the fire are still memories I hold.

---

2 At 5:27 p.m., November 9, 1965, the entire Northeast area of the United States and large parts of Canada went dark. From Buffalo to the eastern border of New Hampshire and from New York City to Ontario, a massive power outage struck without warning. Trains were stuck between subway stops. People were trapped in elevators. Failed traffic signals stopped traffic dead. And, at the height of the Cold War, many thought Armageddon had arrived. One pilot flying over a darkened New York City stated, "I thought, 'another Pearl Harbor!'" By 5:40 p.m. that evening, 80,000 square miles of the Northeast United States and Ontario, Canada, were without power, leaving 30 million people in the dark. blackout@history.gmu.edu

Strawberry Chromosomes and Falling in Love

Alas, I did not return to Camp Mogisca in the summer of 1965. Having finished my first year of teaching at the Thomas School for Girls I felt I should spend a summer gathering laboratory experience. The only laboratory experience I had under my belt was what I learned and experienced at college. Now it was time to discover what "real" scientists were doing and apply what I had learned so far. This would be the "fun" part of my education. I applied to the New England Institute for Medical Research in Ridgefield, Connecticut and was accepted. It was there that I met the man I would marry the following summer.

My first job at The Institute was to mash the bananas and, thus, prepare breakfast, lunch and dinner for the fruit flies' food. The fruit flies, with their four pair of chromosomes, made ideal study creatures. I prepared meals and washed the dishes I had used for the fruit fly nourishment, and continued to prepare meals and wash dishes for the next 16 years but not for fruit flies, for my husband. Some fruit flies came with curly wings and others had straight wings. All had red eyes and yellowish brown bodies. I had no idea what Dr. George Mickey was studying with his fruit flies, but the *Drosophila melanogaster*'s genome wasn't sequenced until the year 2000. Fruit flies mature quickly and mutations can be studied easily. I do remember one day coming into the lab and our mild mannered Dr. Mickey was in a rage. The janitor had hung a Shell Pest Strip outside the fruit fly room and all his flies were dead!

The first day on the job, I asked the gal I was working with if I could join her for lunch. "No," she said, "I will be eating with my fiancé, but I'll introduce you to the fellow next door." So we went into the room where this very attractive young man was studying the chromosomes of strawberries and she said, "This is Lynne. Take her to lunch."

He was taken aback and so was I, but we agreed to meet with our brown bags for lunch at the picnic tables.

I learned immediately that he had just finished his B.S. degree in May of 1965 from the University of Connecticut in the field of genetics and botany. I learned about his family, where he called home and that he would be returning to the University in the fall to finish his Master's work in the field of Cytogenetics. I learned that his passion was not chromosomes; his passion was for hunting and fishing. He was a sportsman who needed a profession to support his hobby. We met for lunch that entire summer. Soon we were going out for dinner, then to the movies, and visiting his folks every week-end. We even took a camping trip to the shore with his family, in a tent! (And my idea of camping is the Marriott!) In fact, we fell in love and got engaged over the summer of 1965, and we were married in 1966.

Neither of us was "churched." As budding scientists, we didn't see the point in organized religion, and I was still angry with the "practical" theology of West Virginia Wesleyan. I did not understand how mandatory attendance at chapel services would make me a religious person? How did tearing down my Christmas door decorations constitute the Christian lifestyle? Why did the Christian Education teacher's theology include the exclusion of women as pastors? Why were gays not worthy to get an education? And why did some Christian professors belittle folk like the Unitarians? I had left all that Christian hypocrisy behind me and I was rejoicing in the philosophy of science.

My husband's family never went to church. In order to keep the peace in my parental household, we agreed to be married in the Highland Park Presbyterian Church up the street from where my parents and siblings lived on Peebles Road. We were married July 2, 1966.

During the summer of 1966, my husband worked again at the Institute, this time studying the chromosomes of gladioli from the farm of Henry Wallace, former Vice President under Roosevelt.

After our honeymoon, we moved into a summer cottage in Ridgefield, CT. My husband went to the lab, and I stayed home. We bought a Beagle puppy and named him Wrinkles. My cat, Desdemona, was completely insulted that we would bring another creature into her life, so she took off. I looked for that cat for days. I went to our one neighbor, Mrs. Miller with an armful of gladioli, and asked her if she had seen a small white and tan cat. No she had not she said, and she shut the door in my face. My husband would often ask me if Mrs. Miller had invited me over, and I always said no. Mrs. Miller had been very attentive to my husband during the month of June when he was living at the cottage by himself and I was home in Pittsburgh making wedding plans. Another day I went over to Mrs. Miller's house and this time I took a photo of Desdemona with me. Mrs. Miller stood at her door, told me she had not seen my cat and then said, "By the way, when are you going to get married?" I was shocked! "Why, we were married July 2nd of this summer," I said. Suddenly, the lady was so polite; she invited me in, she hoped I played tennis, asked if I played bridge and continued to gush all over me. The poor woman thought that we were just "shacking up" for the summer and now she was repentant and wanted to be friends. I just smiled, left and said to myself, "to heck with her, she was, as the old saying goes, 'a day late and a dollar short.'" Mrs. Miller had been rude to me for over 8 weeks. I didn't need a tennis partner now. My husband and I would always refer to that episode as "Mrs. Miller's Regrets."

The first Thanksgiving that I spent with my husband's family was during the year of our engagement. The dinner was fabulous, the usual turkey and trimmings, but also there was ham and venison, oyster stew and New England Succotash. When it was time for dessert, my future mother-in-law asked me what kind of pie I would like and she listed the usual: pumpkin, apple and mincemeat. "Oh," I said, "I'd love some mincemeat pie. My mother makes a hard sauce, do you?" Yes, she did, and I was handed a nice piece of mincemeat pie with hard sauce made with a hint of brandy. I took my first bite, and now I was in trouble. What was I to do? Whatever it was in my mouth was not anything I had ever tasted before. The texture was different but I was there to impress my beloved's mother. Somehow, I swallowed and said, "How do you make your mincemeat pie?" And she said, "First you start with a woodchuck." I was in such shock. All I could say was, "Well, my mother starts with a jar."

Over the 16 years of marriage I learned to cook woodchuck, venison, wild turkey, squirrel, pheasant, rabbit, bear and a sundry of fish, and shellfish. We picked our berries, gathered our eggs, grew our food from an enormous garden, bought our unpasteurized milk from the Lewis farm and generally lived off the fat of the land for most of our married life.

Now, I get all excited when I can go to the store or order from a home delivery service. And, I have never made a mincemeat pie with meat or from a jar. Just think, I had all these experiences, simply because someone at The Institute said, "This is Lynne. Take her to lunch" while he was studying the chromosomes of strawberries and I was mashing up bananas for fruit flies.

PART TWO

Life On Lake Mamanaso Road

Anthony Road

Two Children, One Dog, Two Cars, One Garden,
Two Freezers and Frustration

The Land and Sea Thanksgiving Dinner

Finding My Way Home

Grace

The A-frame House

The Letter!

April Fool's

The Long Walk

Life on The Quad

Here, Kitty, Kitty

Life on Lake Mamanaso Road

My Dad never understood why New Englanders had to name their towns, cities, roads and beaches with names no one from Pennsylvania could pronounce: i.e. Mamanaso and Misquamicut, two of the many places where I have lived. Our Pawcatuck, Connecticut home was not far from the Wequetequock area, made famous by Ruth Buzzi on the 80's TV show *Laugh In*. I should mention that both Pawcatuck and Wequetquock are villages in the town of Stonington, Connecticut.

Recall, Dear Reader, that my husband and I were married in July, 1966 and we were living in Ridgefield, Connecticut for the summer. When September arrived we had to find a place to live within commuting distance to Pine Point School in Stonington, Connecticut where I was to teach, and the University of Connecticut where my husband was to finish his Master's Degree. We found a little "plat/development" house to rent in Norwich, Connecticut. Here we lived for one year with Wrinkles, the beagle.

For the next four years my husband and I lived in Misquamicut, Rhode Island. Here I was introduced to the Winnapaug Pond where we saw sea horses and caught blue-eyed scallops. Up the beach were Weekapaug and Quonochontaug, where we dug for quahogs (clams) which we took home and used in making that famous New England Clam chowder. My Dad just had a fit trying to get used to pronouncing those names, i.e. names which are unknown in Pennsylvania! Instead, in Pennsylvania one can find names such as Licking Creek, Slickville, Slippery Rock and Intercourse, all names that are pronounceable but leave much to the imagination when the original settlers of these places named them.

Those four years at Misquamicut are some of the happiest years of my life. I loved teaching at Pine Point School! My husband was enrolled in a Ph.D. program at Brown University in Providence, Rhode Island. He was able to commute to classes and still find time to explore the ponds and ocean fishing opportunities. I would often accompany him on those adventures. "Spotting" for the Blue-eyed scallops was a new experience for me, but one that I loved. Let me tell you how we did this in Winnapaug Pond, a pond less than a mile from our home on Crandall Avenue in Misquamicut.

My husband had made a "spotter", a wooden box with a glass bottom and open top. This box was about two feet tall and sloped up to the top so that the bottom was about 18 inches square, and the top was about 8 inches square. This arrangement kept unnecessary light out of the viewing box. There were handles attached to the sides of the "spotter" which one held as one looked through the opening down through the box into the water as one walked through the pond. The spotter allowed you to see the scallops either hiding in the mud or water grasses or as they scooted by. Yes, these bivalves can move! The scallop opens its shell and by snapping it closed can move quickly because when the scallop ejects the water that had been in their shell a mini jet propulsion propels the scallop. The mantle, inside the edges of the shell, is covered with blue light sensitive "eyes." The scallop uses its ability to move and to detect light changes to escape from predators such as starfish, crabs and a goony looking woman using her "spotter." Trying to hold the "spotter" with one hand and scooping the scallop with a net with the other hand is quite a feat! My husband made it seem so easy! We never needed to compare our catches because his baskets were always full to the legal limit. But how I loved to take them home, shuck them and put them under the broiler! I went surf fishing with my husband a few times for Striped Bass and Blue Fish. We lived in a fisherman's paradise. My husband was able to unwind from his intensive studies, and I was happily married with a teaching position that fulfilled me in every way. It was a wonderful, fulfilling and romantic four years!

When my husband finished his Ph.D. work he took a post-doctoral job back at the New England Institute for Medical Research in Ridgefield, Connecticut. I don't recall what he was working on this time, but it was neither strawberries nor gladioli. I had to resign my teaching position at Pine Point School and leave behind my colleagues and the friends I had made during the past five years. I found the adjustment of going from a career woman to a stay-at home wife, quite difficult. Unbeknownst to me at the time, our little rented cottage on Lake Mamanasco Road would soon bring a new direction in my life, that direction of being Mother.

My husband came home for lunch everyday. I busied myself getting the Baby's room done. We had no extra money so I tie—dyed sheets using Rite coloring dye in aquamarine and hung these sheets for curtains. I had several baby showers and slowly the room and layette were ready for the new arrival. We had no idea of the baby's gender but we knew we would be excited about whoever arrived. On Sunday, March 14, 1971 Todd was born after a long delivery. He was perfect, and his dad and I were ecstatic.

Neither of us had spent much time with babies, but we figured that two educated people, highly educated in biology and science, would know how to tend to a baby. That is, until the baby came home from the hospital constipated, and we were at our wits' end. We were frantic. We called the doctor. We did just what the doctor said to do: use infant size suppositories. That didn't work! What we were able to help Todd pass were tiny pieces of matter, which appeared to be gravel that cut his little rectum. His dad would cry and I would cry, and of course, Todd was already crying. Then the grandmothers had suggestions: put honey in water; try warm soapy enemas; massage his little belly; give him boiled rice and I don't remember what else we were told. Nothing really worked to give Todd any real relief and his scientifically educated parents were left feeling quite ignorant and guilty that we couldn't solve this problem. At some point, obviously, we were all able to move on . . . no pun intended, or . . . well, maybe!

On Sunday, March 21st, Todd's paternal grandparents arrived. Todd's paternal grandmother's health was still good enough to travel, although her emphysema soon limited her to her own home. The grandparents came bearing gifts for Todd and to see their first grandchild. His birth gift was a Daisy "Red Ryder" BB gun. Somewhere I have photos of this tiny baby and his gun lying in his lap, a gun longer in length than the baby! I don't recall if I were more mystified or horrified, although it was sort of a prophetic gift because Todd grew up to be a total outdoor sportsman, with a love of fishing and hunting. Perhaps Todd's grandparents originated this love of the outdoors with this gift, or it may have been in his genes.

The world of hunting was foreign to me until I met my husband and his family. His family and the extended family were all hunters and fishermen. Most, like Poppa, had a huge garden, a few chickens, and perhaps a cow or pig but the principle protein offered for all meals was meat or fish that someone had shot, trapped, dug, caught, gill-netted or hooked. I had to learn to cook just about everything that swam, ran, flew or crawled in God's great outdoors. So the gift of a BB gun was quite logical to this family, but it sure seemed very strange to me. I was thinking more in line of a silver spoon or a cup, or a sweater or afghan hand knitted by a grandmother. The gun threw me.

When Todd was about 6 months old and his digestive system seemed to be working properly, I had him out in the stroller on the front lawn enjoying the beauty of the September, autumn day, with the reflections of the red and golden leafed trees shining in the lake. Suddenly a van stopped right in front of our house which interrupted and blocked my view. This van had peace signs painted on it that read "Don't trust anyone over 30;" "Hell no we won't go;" "Take your job and shove it;" and other "hippy" and "flower child" epithets and designs. I was appalled, disgusted and outraged—especially since they had messed up that gorgeous view of the Lake. What was a *"peacenik"* van doing in front of my conservative house? As the van drove off, there left behind, by the side of the road, were two very dirty, long haired Flower Children. The van had just dumped them off. I got up to take the baby into the house when one said to the other, "This is the address mother said was hers'." I immediately recognized the voice, dissolving my shock, disgust and outrage. It was my youngest sister, Martha! I hadn't seen her in several years. I recognized her voice, but I had not recognized her. Up the hill the pair came. Martha said that the fellow was her husband, Dale, and they had hitch hiked from California to see the baby. I didn't even know that she had married. I didn't know she had been in California. And hitch hiked! The shock returned, only this time with a grain of incredulity! "You mean you came across country?" I said in disbelief. "You hitch hiked? Isn't that dangerous?" And Martha just smiled and said, "You meet the nicest people, just like those folk in the van, they went out of their way to bring us to you."

I got everyone inside. I telephoned my husband and told him "You better get home early for lunch. Have I got a surprise for you!" I found something for them to wear while I insisted that I wash their clothes. They hadn't seen a shower since heaven knows when. Martha's life style was as foreign to me as if she had come from Mars. We are 10 years apart, and while I was finishing up college and starting my teaching career, Martha got caught up in the anti-war ferver of the 60s and joined with countless other youths in the "Hippie movement." This was a crusade, or a "movement", if you will, embracing drugs, sex, and countless ways to show their disapproval of the establishment, especially over the Vietnam War. In this case, I was the establishment.

I had nothing special to feed them and no car to go to the store, so I heated up the New Brunswick stew that I had made the night before. Since they both declared that yes, they were hungry, but they were **vegetarians,** I served the stew thus:

I added water and made the stew into soup. Then, I carefully picked out the pieces of meat and put those into my husband's bowl and served each of them with what appeared to be a vegetable soup. Dale's hair was as long as Martha's and so we had two ravishingly hungry young people at the table, faces bent over their bowls, hair hanging down the sides of their faces providing a screen around the bowl. I could hear Dale slurping his soup, and then a hand would appear with the bowl and a mumbling, hair muffled sound that he wanted more. Martha was saying things like, "Didn't I tell you my sister was a good cook?" Slurp, slurp, slurp, more, more, more. My husband and I just looked at each other. These folk were darn near starved! We polished off the stew/soup, all the bread in the house, whatever cookies I might have had, or chips . . . whatever I could find to fill these two up, before we could have any conversation. It is a meal I shall never forget. Martha still remembers it as well . . . a meal that was one of her best she'll still declare. And it wasn't until years and years later that I said, "The New Brunswick Stew turned into soup was made with squirrels."

Anthony Road Two Children, One Dog, Two Cars, One Garden, Two Freezers and Frustration

The year of post doctoral work at the Institute was over; my husband was offered a research position at a pharmaceutical company in Connecticut, which he accepted, so we had to move, again! Our fourth move in five years. But this time we were moving to our very own HOME. It was located on Anthony Road in North Stonington, Connecticut. I recall this home with great joy and satisfaction because it was our first purchased home. It came with a manicured lawn, several varieties of fruit trees, a huge overgrown raspberry patch, a back yard with room for a large vegetable garden, and this entire property was surrounded by fields and active farms. I looked out my front, side and back windows and could see cattle grazing everywhere. We had grazing fields across the street from us, and on both sides and to our rear—we were surrounded. When I had to chase a wandering cow out of our garden, then I was none too happy living next door to cows, but overall, our home on Anthony Road was a sweet little place to call our own.

One of the first "improvements" my husband made to the property was to create an enormous vegetable garden. In order to improve the quality of the soil he needed to add manure. We had sufficient sources of what was needed at the neighbors, especially at the Beriah Lewis Farm with their large dairy herd. One year the garden was enriched by a truck load of mackerel. My husband had been out fishing and caught far more mackerel than any household could use, but with his philosophy of "waste not—want not" he brought a truck load home and dumped them in the garden and roto-tillered them under. What a sight! Pieces of tails and heads and bodies were sticking up from the garden. A new crop! I always thought that manure stunk, but this was much worse. We had a crop that stunk! But we had wonderful soil and a bumper crop of beans, tomatoes, peas, broccoli, squashes, pumpkins, mush melons, cucumbers, Brussels sprouts, asparagus, onions, carrots and potatoes that year. We always had apples, pears, strawberries and raspberries that my husband cultivated and nurtured from the property. With venison, wild turkey, fish, scallops, oysters, clams, eggs from our chickens and ham from the pig we shared with Poppa, we didn't lack for much in the food department!

What I lacked was the help with the children and the processing and preserving of all this bounty. My husband believed that he was the one to provide and I was the one to tend to all the domestic chores. My husband was a gifted gardener and he learned from his father who always had large and thriving gardens. My mother-in-law, in turn, did the canning, salting, and freezing: the "putting by" of the harvest. I had watched my mother "can" tomatoes and beans, but until we were ensconced in our home on Anthony Road, I had never tried my hand at canning and preserving tomatoes, beans, peas, or making pickles. I suddenly was on a fast learning curve! Once the harvesting began, I was faced with bushels and bushels of produce.

During the months of August and September I would have a toddler hanging onto one leg while I was boiling water, peeling tomatoes and brining cucumbers. I would often work late into the nights. We needed two freezers to accommodate the harvest of fruits, vegetables, fish and game and the domestic meats that we acquired from a variety of sources. The frustrations and downside were that I had no family or friends to come and help me with what I felt were overwhelming chores. Today, I rejoice when I can go to the store and buy a can of tomatoes, a jar of apple sauce or a bottle of pickles and pick up my beans at the freezer department!

I recall one day when my husband went off to work and he said, "The Brussels sprouts are ready and maybe we could have those for dinner." I grew up hating Brussels sprouts, miniature cabbages that stunk when cooking and tasted about as badly as they smelled. I had never seen how Brussels sprouts grow. But I went out to the garden with Todd in tow and we looked for baby cabbages growing from the soil. We found none! We truly looked very hard. So for dinner that night we did not have Brussels sprouts and my husband was somewhat miffed. When I told him I couldn't find them in the garden he marched me out and showed me! There they were, baby cabbages growing in a spiral array on the side of a long thick stalk of greenery. As mother would say, "If it were a snake it would have bitten you!"

I recall the year my husband planted asparagus. Poppa had the very best asparagus in the world! His patch was so big that when the harvest was over and no one could eat another bite, Poppa would simply cut the asparagus ferns down with his tractor! We wanted an asparagus patch too. So my husband took some one-year old crowns (roots) of asparagus from Poppa's garden and planted them in our garden, giving them all the nourishment, water and sunlight they would need. He told me not to expect to harvest any spears our first year because we had to let them grow and flourish. Maybe by the third year we could truly harvest asparagus. Three years! Oh well, we always had Poppa's asparagus to eat. One day Todd and I went to Poppa's farm and brought home asparagus for dinner. Several of the spears were at least two inches in diameter and just as tender as could be. I took several of those spears and "planted" them in the asparagus patch and then when my husband came home that night I rushed him out to the garden saying, "You'll never believe how the asparagus has shot up over night!" At first sight he believed, but only for a second and then he laughed and said, "You know nothing about Brussels sprouts but you are a quick study for asparagus!"

On February 3, 1973 our daughter, Rebecca was born. She was born at the Westerly Hospital across the state line in Rhode Island. My parents came from Pittsburgh to stay with us and help with Todd while my husband and I were at the hospital. In those days, the mother and child stayed in the hospital for at least five days after the birth. When Todd was born, I stayed in the hospital a full week!

Our daughter was induced. I guess the doctors had something they wanted to do that week-end so I was told to be at the hospital and they would induce labor. As my husband and I and another woman were in the elevator at the hospital and the doors were closed, my husband said to me, "Don't you think we should get married after this baby comes?" I was mortified. I do embarrass easily and now I thought that woman will think we aren't married. Not Mrs. Miller again! My husband just smiled and the doors flew open and I didn't have time to explain to this woman or anyone else that we were married! No one would care one way or the other today!

When we brought baby Rebecca (Becky) home, she was greeted by grandparents, neighbors and Todd. He was 23 months older than the baby and he had been told that a baby was coming to live with him. After several hours of attention being focused on Becky, Todd came over to me carrying her little white sweater and said, "Time to take baby back now." Almost forty years later and there are still many times when Todd wants me to take "baby" back. His world was shattered when Becky arrived. My world was enriched, but it was also complicated. Once my parents left for Pittsburgh and I found myself alone with two children, one dog, two cars, one garden, two freezers, my frustrations grew. I was alone almost every week-end as my husband went ice fishing, or surf fishing, or maybe it was deep sea fishing. And then the hunting seasons: small game like rabbits, squirrels, quail, pheasant, etc., and big game—deer, wild turkey and on and on and on. My husband was providing handsomely for his growing family, and I was struggling with the usual child rearing tasks, domestic duties, and living too far from my parents for any help.

I was overwhelmed, lonely, unhappy and depressed. I missed Pine Point School which was geographically only 7 or 8 miles away in Stonington, but from my perspective, it was just about a world away. I missed adult conversation and intellectually stimulating pursuits. I missed having colleagues and friendships. I missed teaching! Driven by this frame of mind, the children and I one Sunday went to The North Stonington Congregational Church, and my whole life changed and would never be the same again.

As I have watched Becky and my daughter-in-law Trinice handle motherhood, I stand in absolute admiration. They have, from the beginning, shown joy and pure satisfaction in motherhood. They have flourished in their roles as mother. I have told them how proud I am of them. I have also told them that I was so overwhelmed and emotionally unprepared for motherhood that I don't think I ever "enjoyed" those days the way they enjoy their children. So as my reward, I now have four wonderful grandsons to enjoy, pamper and love and when they come to visit and after I have played with them, and I'm tired, they go home!

Meema's Treasures
L to R Back row Lance Meema Robert
L to R front row Mark and Isaac

The Land and Sea Thanksgiving Dinner

We had invited my parents to come and be with us for Thanksgiving. You must know that I was a nervous wreck every time my mother came to visit me. I was convinced that I had to have the house spotless, the children had to be well behaved and the meals had to be done to perfection. Today, as a mother, mother-in-law and grandmother, I know that my "expectations of perfection" were all self induced. I am sure my mother never intended for me to think she was coming to give me the white glove test: but I sure did "sweat the small stuff," the big stuff, and all stuff in general. I would be all tied up in knots by the time she arrived and usually in tears by the time she left. I never felt I had met her expectations of what a wife and mother was supposed to be. I am confessing that those days were hell and they were self inflicted. But the Land and Sea Thanksgiving was a great success and even mother said so.

We decided that we would provide a Thanksgiving meal that was completely from the works of our hands, the land and the sea. My husband was a fabulous gardener, hunter and fisherman. I had "put by" countless jars of pickles, tomatoes, spaghetti sauce, tomato juice, and peaches. In the freezer there were enough beans, broccoli, peas, corn and blueberries for a year. My husband had put in the freezer venison, beef, fresh pork, chicken, rabbit, squirrel, pheasant, duck and sundry species of fish. During the summer, Poppa raised a pig which we shared in feed costs and the men butchered together. We had hams, bacon and fresh pork. When we went to Poppa's farm, I never visited with the pig because I knew its fate and I didn't want to become too friendly. Our next door neighbor, on Anthony Road, was Dave Lewis. He had a dairy farm where we bought all our milk, and we also bought a half of a steer each year. We raised chickens so we had our own eggs. The only things we did not grow, raise, hunt or catch were flour, sugar, coffee, and the various condiments. Other than that we were pretty much self sufficient.

Growing up I learned from my mother how to make bread, cakes, cookies, and pies; how to can, make pickles, jams, jellies, and freeze food. I learned how to cook venison, bear, cod, pheasant, squirrel, rabbit and striped bass from my mother-in-law, Grace, and from various game cook-books. My husband taught me how to dig for clams, spot scallops, catch blue crabs, pull lobster pots, and wrestle oysters off of rocks. I have spent countless hours cleaning crabs, and shucking quahogs, scallops and oysters. The oysters still give me trouble to open! Shucking oysters, Dear Reader, requires a very special kind of knife, and if you try to shuck an oyster with an ordinary knife, you had better wear steel mesh gloves—I learned the hard way.

Thus, with the harvest in, the shelves filled and the freezer full, we saw no reason to buy a turkey and all the trimmings. We had onions, potatoes and carrots in our root cellar, plenty of meat and other vegetables to serve. It was an unusual and memorable meal because there was no turkey and gravy, cranberry sauce or stuffing, or the must have, black olives.

Before I tell you what we served, I want to relate a time when we were at my parents for Thanksgiving and our children were in elementary school. On the drive home, our son, Todd, said something to the effect that he didn't know how I ever managed to grow up with Grandmother and be normal. And then Becky chimed in with, "And I just hated grandmother's pick ass salad." Her father nearly drove off the road from laughing so hard. To this day, aspic salad has been known in our family as "pick ass" salad.

(For the uninitiated: Mother's aspic salad was made with tomato juice, celery pieces and gelatin)

This is what we served for our Land and Sea Thanksgiving Dinner:

Appetizer: tomato juice and oyster stew

Entrees: roasted duck, baked striped bass with onion, tomato and bacon, and hasenpfeffer (a marinated roasted rabbit).

Vegetables: mashed potatoes, carrots with apple (apples from our tree), broccoli with onion and bacon.

Home made bread and a variety of jams and jellies: grape, raspberry, blueberry and apple/quince, all of which I made.

Bread and butter pickles

Apple and Peach pies for dessert.

Mother wrote down the entire menu and said she couldn't wait to share it with her "Prayer and Share" group at church. She was very impressed and excited. Dad said he missed the turkey and asked, "What can we make for sandwiches later without a turkey?" We all agreed the duck was not edible . . . it must have been eating too much pond scum. And, we all decided dinner was a huge success but that next year we wanted a turkey . . . not a turkey from the field, but a turkey from Almacs, Stop and Shop, the A&P, Winn Dixie or any other major grocery store where one can buy a Thanksgiving turkey.

Oyster Stew

- 1/2 cup butter
- 1 cup minced celery
- 3 tablespoons minced shallots
- 1 quart half-and-half cream
- 2 (12 ounce) containers fresh shucked oysters, un-drained salt and ground black pepper to taste
- 1 pinch cayenne pepper, or to taste

Directions

1. Melt the butter in a large skillet over medium heat, and cook the celery and shallots until shallots are tender.
2. Pour half-and-half into a large pot over medium-high heat. Mix in the butter, celery, and shallot mixture. Stir continuously. When the mixture is almost boiling, pour the oysters and their liquid into the pot. Season with salt, pepper, and cayenne pepper. Stir continuously until the oysters curl at the ends. When the oysters curl, the stew is finished cooking. Turn off the heat and serve.

Hasenpfeffer

Ingredients

- 6-8 slices bacon, finely chopped
- 2 rabbits
- 1/2 teaspoon salt
- 1/2 teaspoon black pepper, freshly ground
- 1/2 cup flour
- 1/2 cup onion, finely chopped
- 3/4 cup red wine vinegar (or cider vinegar)
- 1 cup chicken stock
- 1 bay leaf

Directions:

1. Cook the bacon, until crisp. Remove bacon and drain on paper towels. Set the pan with bacon fat aside for a few moments.
2. Cut the rabbit into serving pieces. Cut away and discard the belly meat.
3. Add salt, pepper, and flour to a brown paper bag. Add a few rabbit pieces to the bag and shake to coat with flour mixture; repeat with remaining rabbit pieces.

Preheat the oven to 325 degrees

- In a Dutch oven or heavy bottom Casserole pan add the bacon fat and then brown the rabbit pieces on all sides, in batches, in the bacon fat. Transfer them to a plate and set aside.
- Pour off all but 2 tablespoon of fat and cook the onions in it until they are soft and translucent. Pour in the wine vinegar and chicken stock and add the bay leaf. Bring to a boil over high heat, scraping up any browned bits clinging to the bottom and sides of the pan.
- Return the rabbit with juices to the Dutch oven casserole. Add the drained bacon bits. Cover the casserole tightly, and bake for 1hour, or until the meat is tender but not falling apart.

Finding My Way Home

"Home is the place where, when you have to go there,
they have to take you in."
Robert Frost *Death of a Hired Man*

I hold many fond memories of our place on Anthony Road primarily because this was our FIRST house that we owned and made into a home. I continue to recall with fondness the yard and the fruit trees, the huge raspberry patch, the climbing roses on the trellis outside my kitchen window, the grape arbor and the chicken coop. Now I was NOT fond of going into the chicken coop and putting my hands under the hens to search for an egg or two. I have always been afraid of birds, not birds in the air where they belong, but any loose bird like a parrot, cockatiel or parakeet that someone keeps as a pet. I am very leery of these birds. I don't like being surrounded by pigeons either, so Trafalgar Square in London was not a pleasant experience for me. I cannot bear having sea gulls come up to me or hover over me on the beach and look for a handout. I was chased by a swan once as I was walking across the Weekapaug Country Club greens. I was quite frightened and an angry swan is not to be trusted! Chickens in a pen, minding their own business are quite acceptable. But going into the hen house and collecting eggs always sent my heart into "afib." So when Todd was old enough to walk and carry a basket at the same time, I taught HIM, a darling three year old, to go bravely into the hen house and get the eggs. That was his job. I remember how seriously he took his job and how proud he was when he came to me with his basket of eggs. These are fond memories.

I also hold some not-so-fond memories of Anthony Road life. My Dad had given us his old Buick and so now we had two cars, one for my husband to take to work, and the Buick for me and the children. We had the car for all of two weeks when one day going down to Dave Lewis' dairy to get our milk, the container I used must not have had its lid securely in place. I went around the corner from Boom Bridge Road on to Anthony Road and the milk container fell over on the floor on the passenger side. A gallon of milk spilled over my old "new" car. I did the best I could do to mop up the mess. But until we traded that car in it always stunk of sour milk! Not a particularly fond memory.

If only that was the worst of the memories. Most of my memories during the "Anthony Road" era are a blur as I was so wrapped up in those early years of raising children, tending house, keeping up with diapers and laundry for two toddlers, tending to the harvest in the late summers and early Fall and longing for adult companionship that I was exhausted, unhappy and lonely. I had no women friends or friends my own age with children. We were in the "boonies" and isolated! All of my friends were colleagues at Pine Point. They were working at professional pursuits, and mine were domestic so our lives moved in different directions. I missed teaching. I missed not having a pay check, money of my own. My husband worked hard at the pharmaceutical laboratory all week and he felt, rightly or wrongly, that the week-ends were for his pleasure, his discretion. Boating, hunting, fishing, or going to the family farm kept him busy every week-end.

It is in this frame of mind that I found myself looking for a church to attend. I was looking for a place where I could possibly meet other young women with children. I was looking for a place that offered child care so that I might have one hour to myself in quiet reflection. I was looking for a place that would offer me a safe sanctuary for my thoughts, someplace where I could meditate in peace and quiet. There was a lovely little- white clapboard New England style Congregational Church in the center of our little village of North Stonington. Whenever I had a Sunday when my husband was off somewhere, I took the children and we went to church. The children were little, one a toddler and the other an infant. I only went to church when I had been left alone for the day, but I went often enough that I began to meet other women and I started to look forward to Sunday mornings. Finally, I had someone to talk to.

The congregation had recently called a new pastor, the Reverend Newell Bishop. He took the time to listen to my story, listen to my experience of "leaving" church, and listened to my loneliness. When I told him that a black cloud was constantly following me around and that I was feeling as if it would someday smother me, he compassionately said, "Lynne, you must begin to talk to your husband about these feelings. It is not good for you to hide your feelings and thoughts from him. He can be of no help or consolation if he doesn't know what you are feeling or thinking."

After months of struggling with my sadness and the "black cloud" moods, I tried to tell my husband what I was coping with every day, day after day, and why I was feeling overwhelmed. I will never understand why he responded and reacted as he did, but I will never forget it either. He went into a rage. He ripped the phone from the wall and threw it across the room hitting the glass top of my desk that I had proudly stained and refinished. He told me to pack my bags and go back to my parents' home in Pittsburgh, to get my head straightened out, and that he would take care of the children. Then he stormed out of the house slamming the front door so hard the window broke and he drove off into the night. He was gone for several hours. When he did come home he didn't say a word. He went to bed and went to work in the morning.

I learned that it was not safe for me to ever try to share my inner feelings and concerns with him, especially my needs and most especially, my negative feelings. My husband was a self-centered man, an island unto himself and I felt much neglected. Perhaps that is the reason I returned to religion, returning to what I once knew, the peace and tranquility, the foundation for my personal world, "a place that when you go there they have to take you in." I found acceptance, love, safety, companionship, compassion and intellectual stimulation at the Congregational Church of North Stonington. I made good friends over the years at the church. I remain in contact with some of those women today. I had found my way back, and I was home!

GRACE

"An unexamined life is not worth living."
Socrates

The above words open the book "*I'm Ok, You're OK*" by Thomas Harris, MD which I read in February 1975. I cannot say this book changed my life, but I can say it started me on a frenzy of reading. I began to make notes from this book, and these notes became journals which I kept from February, 1975 through August, 1979. I wanted to record all of the books and articles that I had read, and I was reading. The reading material and the notes that I was making were ways to examine my life. Through those readings I began a spiritual search of myself for the meaning of my life. I was looking for love, for acceptance, for meaning, for fulfillment and for God. The religion that I had been brought up with was no longer working for me; it was dead. It was full of "should have's" and "ought to have's" and a lot of "can't do's." My soul was screaming out to me that for me to return to "church" I needed to be resurrected, if you will, and find myself in a new, life-giving, life-affirming religion. St Paul wrote, "When I was a child, I spoke like a child, I thought like a child, I reasoned like a child; when I became an adult, I put an end to childish ways."[3] As an adult, I needed answers—not just sweet sounding words and phrases! When I went to the church in North Stonington I listened intently to the Reverend Bishop's well thought out and intelligent sermons. And whenever I could find a few uninterrupted moments, I read. Reading has always been my escape, my enjoyment, my transport to places, persons and ideas outside

[3] I Corinthians 13: 11 New Revised Standard Version, 1989

of myself. In my search for meaning, it was a logical thing for me to start with reading.

During the year of 1975 I read some of the popular self-help books such as: *I'm OK, You're OK; I Ain't Much, Baby-But I'm All I've Got* by Jess Lair; and some popular "religious" authors: *Beyond Anxiety* by Bishop James Pike; *A Woman's Choice* by Eugenia Price; *A Second Touch and A Taste of New Wine* by Keith Miller; and *Your God Is Too Small* by J.B. Phillips. My journals are filled with insights and quotes that spoke to me at that time. Soon I was enmeshed with scholarly works that required more effort to understand and apply to my life. I began with Paul Tillich and his *The Shaking of the Foundations.* His chapter entitled "You Are Accepted" did change my life! Let me quote something from the chapter about Grace:

> *"You are accepted. You are accepted, accepted by that which is greater than you, and the name of which you do not know. Do not ask for the name now; perhaps you will find it later. Do not try to do anything now; perhaps later you will do much. Do not seek for anything; do not perform anything;do not intend anything. Simply accept the fact that you are accepted! If that happens to us, we experience grace. After such an experience we may not be better than before, and we may not believe more than before. But everything is transformed . . ."*[4]

Other scholarly works included: *Markings* by Dag Hammarskjold; *On Death and Dying* by Elizabeth Kubler Ross; *How to Believe* by Ralph Stockman; *Dynamics of Faith* and the four volumes of *Systematic Theology* by Paul Tillich; *Credo* by Karl Barth; and *Mere Christianity* by C.S.Lewis. A particular quote from Lewis was also instrumental in my surrender to God and to God's will for my life.

> *"I am trying here to prevent anyone saying the really foolish thing that people often say about Him: I'm ready to accept Jesus as a great moral teacher, but I don't accept his claim to be God. That is the one thing we must not say. A man who was merely a man and said*

---

[4] Tillich, Paul. The Shaking of the Foundations, Charles Scribner's Sons, NY, 1948, pg162.

the sort of things Jesus said would not be a great moral teacher. He would either be a lunatic—on the level with the man who says he is a poached egg—or else he would be the Devil of Hell. You must make your choice. Either this man was, and is, the Son of God, or else a madman or something worse. You can shut him up for a fool, you can spit at him and kill him as a demon or you can fall at his feet and call him Lord and God, but let us not come with any patronizing nonsense about his being a great human teacher. He has not left that open to us. He did not intend to."[5]

Rather than trying to intellectualize and figure out a complete rationale for becoming a Christian I simply stopped and surrendered! If I was feeling neglected and unloved and, therefore, unlovable at home, by my husband, now I knew I was accepted, forgiven, loved and I was loveable by God through Christ. I was ready to "join" the North Stonington Congregational Church and publicly state my faith. I was received into membership in June 1975.

---

5 Lewis, C.S. Mere Christianity. MacMillan Publishing, NY, 1952 pg 55-56.

The A-frame House

We decided to leave the little bungalow on Anthony Road. I cannot recall why we decided to look for another house. Perhaps because we wanted a different school system, or unconsciously thought a move might strengthen our marriage, or we just wanted to be closer to the shore. There were so many factors, some real and practical, and some imagined, reflecting the "hope" that we were experiencing in those troubled times. In any case, we found a unique house on Greenhaven Road in the Pawtucket section of Stonington, Connecticut. The fact that the house was a "modified" A-frame house was exciting. A "modified" A-frame house has walls which differ from a true A-frame house where the steeply sloping roof extends to the ground on both sides, allowing for no vertical wall space. Our home was a two story structure, with side gables and large windows and sliding glass doors on the front of the house. The open living plan included a fieldstone fireplace which extended from the ground floor to the very high ceiling, that is, the height of the house and with a hearth on each floor. The second floor was accessible by a wrought iron spiral staircase which the children were forbidden to climb! On the second floor, which was basically a balcony, there was a sitting room with the fireplace and the master bed and bath. It was a fun house to own. We often watched as people would drive by, stop, gaze and, in some cases, take pictures of this house. We became the proud owners, and Todd began his First Grade at the Deans Mill School in 1977. Becky entered her First Grade in 1979.

By the time we had settled into living on Greenhaven Road, I had become very active at the North Stonington Congregational Church. I was elected a Deacon, I taught an Adult Sunday School class and I had made some very good friendships. Some of the "church" women were also members of the Junior Women's Club and I was asked to join this organization which is part of the General Federation of Women's Clubs. Junior Women's Clubs are for women under the age of 40. The General Federation of Women's Clubs is one of the world's largest and oldest nonpartisan, nondenominational, women's volunteer service organizations, founded in 1890. Our chapter met at the Community Center in Stonington, just a few miles from our new home. Through the club I met more women my age, most of them with children. Thus, between the church and Junior Women's Club, I had ways to serve my community. I now had friends with similar interests. There were couples with which my husband and I could socialize and I was at peace with myself, my home, my family and my God. I was learning and experiencing what it was like to be content. As St. Paul wrote to the church in Philippi, "Not that I complain of want; for I have learned, in whatever state I am, to be content."[6] Paul wrote this while he was chained in jail. I was neither in chains nor in jail. I was living in a fabulous house with two bright and adorable children and a husband who continued to provide for his family in all ways but one, he was emotionally distant from me. Serving Christ, His church and His mission, along with community service through the Junior Women's Club gave me the emotional underpinnings that I needed to be content.

In the "mirror of my mind" one of my best recollections of Greenhaven Road is found in the story of our family rescuing and raising a Canada Goose. When Todd and Becky were ages 7 and 5, we found a day old Canada gosling floating in the Little Narragansett Bay which was very close to our home. My husband and I owned a small motor boat which we used for pulling lobster pots, fishing and Sunday afternoon cruises. It was one of those perfect Sunday afternoons with calm seas and no wind. I was asleep in the cutty cabin and the children were on deck with their Dad, when someone spotted this little bit of fuzz floating in the water. My husband scooped it up with a fish landing net and we brought it home. Then, we called the nature center for advice. They said, "It will die without a community to raise it." Todd, Becky, my husband and I became the community for this little ball of fuzz. Somehow, through a miracle, the little gosling not only lived but he thrived. We called him Honky. I'm sorry we picked that name now, since "honky" is not a politically correct word and whenever I mention this story about our goose and say, "And his

6 Philippians 4: 11. Revised Stand Version, 1946-1952.

name was Honky," people always laugh. We meant no disrespect to white people; we simply named him for the nonstop chatter this creature made. He never stopped his honking. We just loved him. And he, us. He ate with the dog, out of the dog's bowl on the back porch of our A-frame home on Greenhaven Road. He also ate all of my rose bushes. He followed my husband around like a shadow because he could usually count on a few treats that my husband had put in his trouser cuffs. My sister, Martha, always likes to remind me that Canada Geese "are pretty to look at, but their 'pooh' is too big and they honk too loud." I would agree about those two negatives. They are messy to have around so you have to watch your every step, and they are very noisy. But we loved our goose. He was ours!

Honky followed us everywhere. We should have called him "Shadow." He was not allowed in the house, but when we were in the yard, this bird, was attached at the hip with us. Todd taught him to fly. Todd would run in front of him flapping his arms and it didn't take too long before Honky was off the ground.

When a flock of geese flew over the house one autumn day, we were sure Honky would join them. We watched him take off, sounding off "here I come" and we felt somewhat abandoned and sad. Yet, we had hoped that this would happen. Up he went to meet this flock of geese in their traditional V formation. But he was rejected. He didn't belong to their flock. I've often wondered if they had accepted him, perhaps his fate would have been different. You see, I think Honky thought he was a person. He had imprinted on us as a family. He ate and played with our family dog. So he was a very confused creature. He was neither human nor canine and after being rejected by his own kind he had no knowledge of his true identity.

After much thought we decided that the best place for our goose was to take him to a bird sanctuary where he would be safe from predators and perhaps he could learn to be a goose. I don't recall where this sanctuary was but I remember how badly my husband felt after we left him there. The area he was to live in was fenced and had netting over the top, so naturally the goose was going to be confined, but safe. After a time my husband was so agitated thinking about the goose being totally confined, away from everything it knew, that he went back to the bird sanctuary and brought Honky home. We settled back into life as usual, that is, two children, one dog and one goose. Until one morning a neighboring dog came into our yard. Honky went over to say, "hello" just as he had said "hello" to our dog everyday. But this dog didn't know Honky and did what most dogs would do in those circumstances and after a very brief "encounter," our goose was dead. This was a very traumatic moment for us as a family but especially for my husband. He was devoted to this creature. He had a taxidermist mount the bird and he still has it to this day.

Had we done the right thing to bring the goose home in the first place? Had we done the right thing to bring him home a second time? Were we at fault by not adequately protecting him? Were we wrong to encourage him to think he was more human than goose? Were we to blame for his demise? In truth we were not the community which Honky deserved and needed. "Birds of a feather flock together," and we were not his flock. Honky needed the community of a flock of Canada geese in order to truly thrive and survive, no matter how much we loved him and how much he seemed to love us.

This is the basis of the story I have told every congregation I have served. There are lessons we can learn about community from this encounter with one particular Canada Goose. I offer a "traditional" Trinitarian worship service around our story of Honky and the ways of Canada Geese in general: three hymns, three jokes and a three point sermon:

- Know who you are and to whom you belong.
- Know where you are going and how you are going to get there.
- Respond to the encouragement of others and take care of one another.

After this episode we never took in another lost or abandoned creature. But we did learn from our experience as a family and we each hold fond memories of a magnificent Canada Goose named Honky.

The Letter!

It was March 15, 1979 when the letter from Yale Divinity School (YDS) arrived. The Ides of March! One day after Todd's 8th birthday.

I held the letter in my hands for a long time before I opened it. I had applied to YDS in 1978, against the wishes and opinions of my husband, my parents and others. One of the others who did not support me during those discerning months of inner struggle and my application process was an Episcopal priest in Westerly, RI. who believed that God did not call women to the ordained ministry and he told me so. I had taken the Bible study *The Edge of Adventure* with him at his church and during that course I continued to wrestle with the idea that God was calling me, again, into the ordained ministry. I argued with God. "Who me?" I told God. "I have a husband, two children, a dog, two cars, two freezers and my own frustrations enough without adding the complications of going into the ministry." I reminded God that when I was thirteen I tried to commit my life to "full time Christian service" and "as you know, God, that didn't work out at all." I spoke of my inner struggle to my pastor, Newell Bishop, to my Sunday school class, to my closest friends about this "call" which did not seem to make sense to me at this stage of my life.

I came across a devotional titled *Who Me?* that I clipped and saved in my journal. I don't know the name of the author.

Who Me?

And the Lord said, "Go"
And I said, "Who me?"
And He said, "Yes you."
And I said

"But I'm not ready yet
And there's company coming
And I can't leave the kids
And you know there's no one to take my place."
And he said, "You're stalling."
Again the Lord said, "Go."
And I said, "I don't want to."
And he said, "I didn't ask if you wanted to."
And I said
"Listen. I'm not the kind of person
To get involved in controversy
Besides my family won't like it
And what will the neighbors think?"
And he said, "Boloney."
And yet a third time the Lord said, "Go."
And I said, "Do I have to?"
And he said, "Do you love me?"
And I said
"Look, I'm scared
And people are going to hate me
And cut me into little pieces
I can't take it all by myself."
And he said, "Where do you think I'll be?"
And the Lord said, "Go."
And I sighed
"Here I am, send me."

From the Marriage Encounter Newsletter 1977

I may have heard God's voice. But there were other voices telling me I was wrong. My parents were fearful that an endeavor such as returning to school, for any subject, would harm my marriage and harm my children, ages 8 and 6. But the biggest and most important voice was that of my husband of 13 years. He told me flat out that he would not support me financially, emotionally or in any way, if I decided to go to YDS and study, "religious bullshit." "Now, if you are dead set about returning to school, if you have some need to further your studies in biology," he said, "I'll try to be supportive."

I held the letter in my hands for a long time. It was a thin letter. Does that mean I have been rejected? Well, I guess that would be OK, an answer to the negative voices I had been listening to for over a year. And I did finally say to God, "Alright! I'll apply to a seminary, but I doubt I'll ever get into Yale and I'm only applying to Yale!" I was not really expecting to get accepted. However, by the time I had gone through all the hoops and written my essays, and I had an interview with Joan Forsberg, Assistant Dean and Director of Admissions and I had pestered others to write recommendations, I must admit, I wanted to be accepted. It was a very thin letter.

I called my girlfriend, Martha Bradshaw. "Martha, the letter came! I'm still holding it in my hands," I nearly screamed. "Well, open it you silly goose," she said. And so I opened that thin letter, a piece of paper that would be a deciding factor of how my life was to be played out, certainly not knowing the future, but sensing this was to be a momentous moment in my life, one way or the other.

You would think I would have memorized that letter. I didn't. All I can recall is that I was accepted to Yale Divinity School and I could begin in the fall term of 1979. Martha yelled and I yelled and we both cried and then I had to call my pastor, Newell and he yelled and he cried and then I cried. I had to call my Adult Sunday school class which I taught and we all yelled and we all cried. Tears of joy. Shouts of gladness. It was all very overwhelming. I was accepted!

And then reality broke in. How was I to tell my husband? How was I to tell my parents? How was I going to juggle two children and their schedules, the housework, the shopping, the cooking and round trip commute of 130 miles to school? How was I going to pay for this schooling? The letter didn't say anything about financial aid! How was I going to tell my husband?

I don't remember if I called him at his office. Did I wait and tell him when he got home? I don't recall. What I do remember were his words at the dinner table. "I truly wish I could be excited for you."

He wished he could be excited was a better response than what I had imagined. I was satisfied with that response. There were no outbursts, no nastiness, and no ultimata. There was just his wish that he could be excited.

He, of course, never got to the point of being able to be excited about my endeavors to pursue a seminary degree. After two years of my studies, he left the marriage, and that is by far the greatest heartbreak of my life and at the same time, the most liberating.

April Fool's

The symptoms started slowly. Sometimes I just ignored them. Other times I wondered what was wrong with me. I was losing the feelings in my fingers and toes, which caused me to drop things more than usual. My lips had a hard time distinguishing between warm, warmer and hot! I took to drinking anything cold out of the refrigerator or sticking my finger in my coffee cup to test the temperature. Sometimes my words came out all screwy, almost garbled. At times I stumbled like a drunken sailor, although I've never seen a drunken sailor. It is just that I had a hard time walking in a straight line. If I had been pulled over by the police and was asked to touch my nose with my finger or walk a straight line, I think I might have failed the test. And then there were the aches and pains: joints that were so sore I could barely put on my jacket. I was so constipated I cried and thought I might have a hernia trying to relieve the pressure. There was some periodic paralysis in my legs; my health and conditions seemed better some days than others. Something was wrong and I didn't know what. This was in the spring of 1979.

As you will recall I received my acceptance into Yale Divinity School on March 15, 1979. Remember, I mentioned the dichotomy of emotions I had at that time. I was trying to balance the sheer joy of acceptance and the terror of my husband's rejection. I rejoiced with my friends from church and secretly cried that I would never find the funds or the time to make the acceptance a reality.

Were these symptoms caused by fright and terror? Should I seek a psychologist? Were these symptoms caused by some bacterium or virus? Should I seek out my internist?

I chose the latter and my internist did a simple test with a pin, jabbing me in all parts of my body and asking, "Do you feel this, do you feel that?"

From the results of the simple pin test, I was sent to a neurologist in New London, CT. I don't remember his name. But I remember he used the same pin test and announced that I was to be admitted to Lawrence and Memorial Hospital for a spinal tap.

So off we went to the hospital. My church friends had made a large card and everyone had signed it. It sat on the little night stand next to my hospital bed. My husband stayed until "lights out," kissed me good night and promised to be back the next day for the test.

I really had no idea what a spinal tap entailed. I was a compliant patient. I asked very few questions and because I was raised to believe that doctors were to be considered gods, I never questioned why a spinal tap was ordered or what the doctor was looking for from the test.

A spinal tap is a procedure performed on the patient when a doctor needs to look at the patient's spinal fluid. I was on a table that tilted from the horizontal to the vertical so that my body might be upright, or upside down. I don't remember all the prep work. I was dressed in hospital issued pajamas. I remember lying on my stomach and strapped to the table, the table tilted and I was facing down, looking at the floor. I was surprised!

I hadn't known I would be going on a see saw ride. I gripped the steel table in fear. Next the table tilted in the opposite direction and now my feet were headed to the floor and my pajama bottoms started to fall down. I grabbed for the pajamas. I heard the nurses and everyone else in the room yell **"STOP,** you have a needle sticking in your spine. Move and you will end up paralyzed!" Now they tell me. When I recall that moment and think I could have been paralyzed over a sense of modesty, I still react with amazement. Why don't doctors tell their patients everything before the fact? I have learned over the years to ask questions. But even so, there are still times when I am taken aback by my lack of knowledge and the failure on my part to ask questions and the doctor's part to explain procedures.

So my spinal fluid was extracted. I was returned to my room where I was to lie flat for many hours so as to avoid a headache. My husband was waiting for me in the recovery room as promised. I spent the day resting and lying flat and then I was released. But before I was released, in came the doctor and said without much fanfare or "bedside manner," "My preliminary study of the spinal fluid shows a higher concentration of something, (I don't recall) and "I am pretty sure you have Multiple Sclerosis (MS). You will have to make an office appointment and we can talk further." This diagnosis happened on April 1, 1979. No fooling!

No joking! 16 days after I received the letter of acceptance from YDS, I received this devastating news. What kind of celestial joke was that?

Needless to say, by the time our visit with the neurologist came about I had plenty of questions! And so did my husband. After the doctor assured us this was not Lyme disease, which he had originally suspected, he proceeded to tell us about MS. He told me to stay away from any MS support groups; they would only make me depressed. He said that there was no predicting how the disease would play out. He also said that this disease could go into remission and I would have no other episodes. The Doctor started me on prednisone, an anti-inflammatory drug. I am sure we talked about lots of things, but I can only remember quite clearly my husband saying to the doctor, "Lynne has been accepted to the Yale Divinity School starting in September. I don't see how she can go now, do you?" And the doctor said, "If she were my wife, I would encourage her to do as much as she can; whatever she is able to do, and let her be the one to decide." I wanted to kiss his feet, but only thought "God bless him." I can't remember his name. But I remember his answer.

I went home determined that I would learn everything I could about this disease and how I would live with it, if I had to.

The Long Walk

I was 37 years old when I was diagnosed on April 1, 1979 as having many of the classic symptoms of Multiple Sclerosis. These symptoms included problems with balance, eyes, bowels, pain, paralysis and fatigue. My children were 8 and 6, and I know they were worried when they saw their mother struggling, sometimes with a cane and other times just plain too exhausted to be "mother." When I returned from the hospital after the spinal tap and made the appointment with the doctor for the follow up, my legs were giving me the most trouble. I can remember one day lying on the sofa and deciding that I had to go get the mail out at the mailbox. Somehow I had built up in my mind that if I didn't get the mail, I may never get off the sofa again, literally and figuratively. It was a struggle! It took me several hours to get out to the mailbox at the end of the drive and back to the sofa. But I made it! It is hard to explain the significance of that trip to the mailbox.

The children were off to school, my husband had gone off to work and I was all alone: frightened and mad. I was mad at God. How could this happen to me? God knew the emotional and spiritual struggle I had gone through to even apply to a theological school and God knew how I had wrestled with that decision. It had caused me to have insomnia and kept me up at night. I didn't want to jeopardize my marriage. I didn't have access to any marital funds. I had had serious doubts about my chances for completion of the theological program, and I didn't expect to even succeed in getting accepted even if I did apply, so why waste the time and energy and application fee? I struggled over all of that. And then God smiled on me, and I did get accepted. And now this! I was barely able to get off the sofa and walk out to the mailbox and get the mail. How in heaven's name was I ever going to get to go to Yale come September? Yes, I was mad at

God. If it is true that God's eye is on the sparrow and the hairs of my head are all counted (Matthew10: 29-30) then why was this happening to me when I was trying to answer the call, "Come, follow me."

I had been part of a *Faith at Works* group held at a Church in Westerly. When the Associate Minister, who facilitated the group, heard that I had been diagnosed with MS he said to one of the members of our group, "This is God's punishment. Women have no business trying to enter the ministry." When my friend told me what the good reverend said I only got angrier. I didn't really believe that God punished people with diseases but the reverend's unkind remarks set in motion a brief period of doubt, should I be pursuing this call? Was I being punished? Was this a way to say I had misinterpreted God's leadings?

I couldn't and didn't answer all those deep theological and existential questions that afternoon. What I did do was really more important at the time. I got myself out to the mailbox and back. I carried a chair to the door and using the chair as a walker, I pushed the chair down the stony driveway, stopping after a step or two and then sat in the chair. I waited for some strength and dried my tears from the pain and then I would push a little further. Push, sit, wait: push, sit, wait until I got to the road. Look both ways . . . push, sit wait . . . but not too long, stand, get the mail, sit, catch your breath and head back across the road and down the driveway which seemed like miles to go. I did it! I cannot explain the feeling of accomplishment and satisfaction. Even today, I wonder what the outcome would have been if I had not tried or if I had tried and failed: would I still be on the sofa? That short walk was symbolic, it was prophetic—I walked to freedom that day, when I was 37 and the children were 8 and 6 and I was mad at God.

Life on the Quad
1979-1983

Academic vigor, a faith community to engage with, and a place where my faith and my intellect were nourished all contributed to my life on the Sterling Divinity Quadrangle of the Yale Divinity School in New Haven, Connecticut. Those years on "the Quad" were the most exciting, most demanding, and most spiritually enlightening years of my life. You will recall, Dear Reader, that my years in High School and College were years of great disappointment. My academic work was satisfactory, but I always felt out of place, left out of the social aspects of High School and college life and I was quite lonely during those earlier school days.

But not so at YDS! I thrived on the studies, the worship services at Marquand Chapel, the commute and camaraderie and friendship that I shared with Mary Yanaway and two other women from the Stonington/ Groton/ Eastern Connecticut area. I spent hours in the magnificent library on campus, reading and studying for my classes. The subjects that I was taking were taught by some of the world's finest scholars in theology, sacred scripture, the history of Christianity and ethics. I also studied under the tutelage of outstanding professors of homiletics, pastoral care, and Christian education. During my four years at YDS I took courses offered by such "greats" as Letty Russell, Luke Timothy Johnson, Henri Nouwen, Brevard Childs, Bonnie Kittel, Margaret Farley, William (Bill) Muehl, Gaylord Noyce, Gene Outka, Robert Johnson, Richard Hays, Rowan Greer, Hans Frei, and Randolph C. Miller. Leander Keck was our Dean and Joan Forsberg was an Associate Dean, and she was also a friend and a shoulder to cry on.

I remember one day when I was at home writing and typing yet another paper and Becky said, "Mommie, I thought you were going to school to become a preacher, but all you do is type." Yep, I did a great deal of typing on the same Smith Corona electric typewriter that I had taken to college in 1960. I had to use carbon paper when I needed a duplicate copy and then often used "white out" for the countless mistakes I would make in typing. We also used onion skin, in those days, to make copies. Do you remember onion skin? Well, then, you must remember that it does not erase well, and white out sticks out like a sore thumb. As an aside, I upgraded to a Brother Word Processor by the time I started my doctoral work in 1994. It was a big step forward, but I was still computer illiterate at that time. How did we ever manage without computers?

How did I ever manage to graduate from YDS? Only by the grace of God! When I first started, I registered for my first and only class in the fall semester of 1979. At that time I did not know anyone from my area that was commuting by car to New Haven. My legs were too shaky from the bout with MS to drive by myself so I took the train. Once I arrived in New Haven, I would hire a taxi to take me to 409 Prospect Street. Using a walking cane, I would go through the white gates that opened on to the Sterling Divinity Quadrangle. What a beautiful panorama the eye beheld: a center green that sloped up to the Marquand Chapel. On each side of the green were red brick buildings with huge brick columns matching the color and brick of the Chapel. These buildings were used for offices and the Divinity library. The quadrangle was beautiful all seasons of the year, but in the fall of 1979, with all that I had been through just to get there, I was especially overwhelmed. The sight brought tears to my eyes. I was living out a dream, a dream I never believed would become real.

I signed up for only one course that first semester in order to see if I could handle the train commute, the academics and also balance my home responsibilities. I decided to take as my first course, Pastoral Counseling, taught by Toni Smith. It was a rigorous course because we had to conduct many "interviews" and each of which had to be audio-taped. Then a verbatim transcript, with annotations had to be produced and turned in. This course was emotionally draining as well as tedious. I received an excellent grade for that course. Also taking Pastoral Counseling was another first year student, Mary Yanaway, from the neighboring town of Noank, Connecticut. From the second semester through graduation,

Mary and I commuted together. A friendship developed, and we had each other to study with during our commute.

I was always amazed when the younger students would ask the professor for an extension on the due date of their papers because "they were too busy." Mary and I and all of the other "second career" students were also busy: busy with family responsibilities, busy commuting, busy with our internships, and, in my case, busy working as an Activities Director at the Watch Hill Nursing Home. So I knew busy! My health improved every year, so that by my final year in 1983 I no longer needed or used a cane, and I was driving as part of our car pool.

As I mentioned, I was part of the "second career" student population. Our classmates represented a diversity that was rich in ethnic and racial backgrounds, sexual orientations, marital status and denominational affiliations. Those of us women who were second career students carried our books in canvas bags, and those students who had recently graduated from college carried their books in back packs. We were affectionately referred to as "The Bag Ladies."

The interchange of ideas from the rich diversity of the student body was stimulating to my faith and to my intellect. Because YDS is an ecumenical, university-based divinity school I was exposed to a variety of religious practices as expressed within the various denominations represented at the school. We were also encouraged, as students, to take courses from the other professional schools connected to Yale University and to utilize the many libraries on campus. I particularly enjoyed the Beinecke Rare Book and Manuscript Library where the Gutenberg Bible is on permanent display. This is the library's oldest western work printed from moveable type by Johann Gutenberg in about 1454. When you stand in the center of the Beinecke library you are bathed with light that passed through the marble window panes, light that will not damage the collection of books and manuscripts, light that seems "other worldly." My life at YDS those four wonderful years seemed, then, and even now, as "another world," a world set apart, a holy world!

Let me say a brief word about finances. When I was accepted by YDS, I was married but I had no access to my husband's money. In other words, there were no "marital funds" for schooling. He told me outright that he would not financially help me to go to a school to study something "of dubious worth." I went to my Savings and Loan bank and borrowed $2500. That money helped me with my books, train and travel expenses and course work for the first semester. I proved myself that first semester, and I received financial aid from YDS. I was given scholarships from the New London Association of the United Church of Christ, awarded the Lizzie Dolbeare Scholarship for four years, and received monetary gifts from friends and the North Stonington United Church of Christ. It was by God's grace that my four years on the Quad only cost me $2500. An amazing feat!

Graduation was on May 23, 1983. My parents, and my son and daughter, Todd and Becky, were in attendance. It was a thrilling day. One of the honorary doctoral degrees given that day was to Meryl Streep who had graduated from Yale Drama School in 1975. I don't recall who the principal speaker was; I was excited to see Meryl Streep. The undergraduate degrees and the degrees from the 10 professional colleges were given out at the individual colleges. At the Divinity School our class stood, as a class, for the last time in the Quad waiting to hear our names read, hear the degree that was earned, and then we walked up the four or five stairs in front of Marquand Chapel to receive our degree . . . written in Latin. My diploma from YDS is my most cherished document, and yet I do not have it framed. It rests securely in my "hope chest," a present that was given to me long ago by my former husband, the one person I had hoped would be there for me. By the time I graduated my children were 14 and 12, I had a job as the pastor of the First Baptist Church of North Stonington, Connecticut, my health was improving, my parents were supportive and proud of my accomplishments and I was proud of myself, as well. How did I ever do it? By the Grace of God!

Here, Kitty, Kitty

It seemed like an ordinary day, so ordinary that I cannot recall the day or even the month, but the year was 1981. It was such an ordinary day! I had gotten the children off to school, my husband had left for work and I had things to do: you know, laundry, shopping and the usual. However, I didn't have to be in New Haven for school that day, nor did I have to be at Pine Point where I taught one course or the Pendleton Hill Church, where I was serving as Student Pastor. The day was mine to cram everything into it that was possible while my usual schedule was otherwise so full. I started the laundry and went grocery shopping.

When I came back to the house, my husband was home. This was not ordinary. He never came home early. He seemed angry that I was not home when he had arrived and said he had been calling all morning. There were no cell phones in those days! But when he saw I was carrying in groceries he said, "Oh, now I know where you were." He went upstairs and said, "When you're finished putting away the groceries, come up because I want to talk to you." This was not ordinary, but I didn't think too much about it. I finished putting the groceries away and went up the spiral staircase to our bedroom. We were living in the A-frame house in Pawcatuck at the time. He was lying on the bed and he didn't look well.

"Are you sick?" I said. "No" he replied, "I came home to give you this letter." And he handed me a letter which I still have tucked away in a very safe place. I sat down on my side of the bed and read the letter which basically stated his opinions of the children and their needs and his unhappiness with the marriage. One sentence read, "Not all of this is your fault." It took many years to figure out that not everything was my fault but that my husband's basic emotional and other needs would never be met by me or any other woman.

So I sat there with this letter and said something . . . I have no idea and cannot, to this day, remember what I said. I just recall that my husband said he needed time to think; he was moving out and he would come back later, on the week-end, and get some of his things that he really wanted, particularly his bureau and gun cabinet. He packed his bags with clothes and left. Just like that! On an ordinary day in an ordinary month in the year 1981, he came home, handed me a letter and was gone. I was in shock!

Now, years before when we took in a stray cat, my husband had said he didn't want the cat in the house. I liked the cat and, of course, I wanted the cat in the house. But, in an effort to be cooperative and sympathetic to his desires, I didn't let it in. However, I had said to him in jest, "The day you move out is the day the kitty moves in." That was years before this letter and my husband's leaving . . . never to return.

But on that day, after my husband went out the front door, I went to the kitchen door and said, "Here, Kitty, Kitty."

PART THREE

A Conversation at the Soccer Field

My arrival at The First Baptist Church of North Stonington, commonly known as the Pendleton Hill Church, was one of many miracles in my life. The year was 1981. I had returned to Pine Point School as a part-time science teacher prior to my acceptance at Yale Divinity School (YDS). My schedule at Pine Point was very limited, but I was happy to be back in the classroom and among former colleagues and friends. One day, as I was watching a soccer game, the Reverend Richard "Dick" Mitchell came up to me and we talked. Dick had been appointed interim Head Master of Pine Point and he was hoping the trustees of the school would ask him to be the permanent Head Master. Dick was also serving as the part-time pastor of this little American Baptist church, a/k/a Pendleton Hill Baptist Church in North Stonington. Dick and I had known each other since 1967 when he and his wife, Linda, first came to teach at Pine Point and I was the chair of the science department.

Dick and I shot the breeze, so to speak, for awhile and then Dick told me how important the little church was to him. He didn't want to give up the Pendleton Hill church while he was interim Head Master for fear that if the trustees did not ask him to be Head Master he would be without the headmaster job and the church as well. So his proposal was thus: I could do my YDS required "field placement" as a student pastor at Pendleton Hill and Dick would be my supervisor. We could and would share the preaching duties. I would cover all the visitation and administrative duties and he would perform the marriages and funerals. This idea intrigued and excited me. This would be a way for me to accomplish several things at once: I would have my required student ministry work covered and I would gain church experience working with an experienced pastor and dear friend. I hoped that the folk on my "United Church of Christ In-Care

Committee" did not mind that I would be working in a Baptist Church and not a United Church of Christ (UCC) institution. I told Dick to go ahead and ask the powers that be at Pendleton Hill if this proposal would work for them, and I would check with my UCC In-Care Committee and YDS. I am pleased to report that everything fell into place, and everyone was pleased and cooperative.

An interesting part of this story is that three days before my conversation at the soccer field I had had an interview for my student field placement at the Women's Prison in Niantic, Connecticut. That conversation went something like this:

Chaplain: This is a Woman's Prison but the position that is available to a seminarian is for an assistant chaplain in the secured prison for the men here at Niantic. Have you any experience working with inmates?
Me: No.
Chaplain: Have you any experience working with men?
Me: No.
Chaplain: Have you any experience working with urban men?
Me: No.
Chaplain: Good, you will make a great associate. When do you want to start?
Me: Let me think about it and I'll get back to you.

I suppose the chaplain offered me the student position because I had no experience and no preconceived ideas about prison life. I could be easily trained by the chaplain. I was flattered that I passed the interview, but I was really very nervous about doing my field placement in a prison, especially for a secured prison. So when Dick proposed that he and I become the dynamic duo at Pendleton Hill I was thrilled! The good folk at Pendleton Hill did not want to lose Dick but they understood that his new position at Pine Point would be very demanding and my presence at the church, as a staff member would help him. They also liked the idea that they would be part of, and participating in, a student's religious life and growth. Thus, in September of 1981 I officially began my ministry at an American Baptist church in North Stonington, three miles up the hill from my home church, The North Stonington Congregational Church, UCC.

Dick was called to be the Head Master of Pine Point sometime in1981 and he served in that role until 1990. Dick resigned his pastorate at Pendleton Hill in 1982 but retained his membership there. By vote of the congregation I began my Pastorate at Pendleton Hill Church on September 1, 1982 and I held that position until July, 1989.

Everything was a "first" for me at Pendleton Hill: officiating for my first wedding service, my first baptism, my first funeral, my first communion service, my first everything! This congregation was a loving and welcoming group, in a lovely rural setting. The congregation was very accepting of a student who was still learning and growing into her first role of pastor. The congregation at the Pendleton Hill Church was small but very devoted to Christ, His Church and His mission. This congregation saw me through the final years of my schooling and supported and consoled me through my divorce. This congregation taught me what it is to be a healthy church, a place where we laughed, prayed, and worked together for the glory of God. We shared each other's burdens as well as each other's joys. This was the perfect congregation to teach a seminarian how to become a pastor.

Ecumenical Ordination Held For Pastor of Pendleton Hill Baptist Church[7]

My ordination was a grand affair. On the 23rd day of October 1983 an ecumenical gathering of ministers, church members and my entire family came together to celebrate my call to ministry and to ordain me to the Christian Ministry by prayer and the laying on of hands. We gathered at the Pendleton Hill Baptist Church for the ceremony, and then the entire congregation traveled down Wyassup Road to The North Stonington Congregational Church for the reception. You see, I was ordained into the Christian Ministry for the United Church of Christ (UCC) and also into the Christian Ministry for the American Baptist Churches, USA (ABC/USA). This dual ordination was a historic event, and to my knowledge no one in Connecticut, before this auspicious occasion, had ever been ordained by two different denominations at the same time on the same day, with dignitaries and representatives of the denominations present in the same place. This is how it happened.

When it came time to prepare for my Ordination Council, sometimes referred to as the Ordination Examination, I was "In-Care" of the New London Association of the UCC. The purpose of the ordination examination is to determine the preparation and fitness of the candidate for ordination in and on behalf of the UCC. Ordained ministers and delegates from the churches which make up the particular UCC Association gather to hear the ministerial candidate read a paper and answer any questions the members of the council may have. I asked: "Would it be possible to have

---

7 Jean North. *The Sun*, "Ecumenical Ordination Held For Pastor of Pendleton Hill Baptist Church" Westerly, RI Friday, October 28, 1983 pg. 4.

an Ordination Examination for the New London Association and also seek to have an Ordination Council with the American Baptist Association?" The UCC Association members responsible for my "In-Care" status answered: "It has not been done before, but there is no reason for us to say you cannot. You will have trouble with the Baptists!" They also said, "You will have to prove you took a polity course about the United Church of Christ."[8] I had taken my UCC polity course at YDS.

Armed with the UCC approval, I went to the Stonington-New London Association of the American Baptist Churches and asked the same question: "Could I have an Ordination Council with this Association since I was already serving an American Baptist Church as Pastor?" Their answer was: "First, you will need a polity course for the American Baptist Churches," (which pleased me because I had done this as a private student with the Reverend James Pratt who taught polity at YDS). Then they also said, "It has never been done before, but there is no reason not to allow a dual ordination since you are presently serving one of our churches. But, you will have trouble with the UCC!" I had no troubles with either denomination.

I read my Ordination Paper for the UCC Council at the North Stonington Congregational Church one Sunday afternoon and read the identical paper the following Sunday at the American Baptist, Pendleton Hill Church. My Ordination paper was, like all candidates for ordination

---

[8] **Church polity** is the system of government used by a given church. Among most types of churches, we find three types of polity: *episcopal, presbyterian* or *congregational.*

episcopal polity is the polity in which bishops (Greek: episkopos) rule.

presbyterian polity is the polity of churches governed by a "session" (council) made up of the minister(s) and lay elders. The session is under the presbytery, which is a body made up of representatives from member churches. Likewise the synod is over the presbytery and the General Assembly is over the synods.

congregational polity technically is a polity in which the individual congregation is completely autonomous in rule. Most congregational polity churches do cede some authority to higher level groups. Baptists are the best known congregationalists in polity today, but the original American congregationalists were known simply as the Congregationalists and they are now part of the United Church of Christ.

of both the ABC/USA and the UCC, a statement of my theological perspective and grasp of the historic Christian faith. In this paper I had to demonstrate my knowledge and understanding of the history, theological roots, polity and practices as they related to the faith and practice of the Church, as well as to my own pilgrimage of faith and understandings of and the intentions for my ministry. I had to state my vision for ministry and document an official "Call" to a particular ordained ministry. My official "Call" was my position as Installed Pastor of the First Baptist Church of Pendleton Hill, commonly known as The Pendleton Hill Baptist Church.

After I finished reading my paper and answering the various questions put forth to me, I was given a standing ovation at BOTH councils! I, however, was not standing. I read my paper seated on a high stool because I still did not have the strength in my legs to stand for any period of time due to the symptoms of the MS.

And that is how it happened that on Oct 23, 1983 I was ordained into the Christian ministry by both the ABC and the UCC. I had asked close friends to read scripture and take part in the worship service. Martha Sweitzer played the organ. Martha was a retired music teacher at Pine Point. The Reverend Richard "Dick" Mitchell, Head Master of Pine Point School and former Pastor of Pendleton Hill, took part by leading us in prayer. The Reverend Newell Bishop from The North Stonington Congregational Church gave "The Charge" to me, and The Reverend James Pratt, Baptist Polity lecturer at YDS and Pastor of the Noank Baptist Church, gave "The Charge" to the Congregation. My brother, Ted, spoke on behalf of our family. I held my breath that whatever stories and jokes he would tell would be suitable for the occasion. They were! He was great and I was proud of him as he affirmed my call to ministry pledging the service and support of our family. The sermon was given by The Reverend Virginia Sullivan, pastor of the Dunn's Corners Community Church, Presbyterian in Westerly, RI. Virginia was the first woman pastor that I had met. We would visit together, and I would pepper her with questions about ministry and gender, family acceptance and academics. She came to Dunn's Corners in the 1970s and retired in 1988. An interesting aside, Virginia became the Pastor at the Pendleton Hill Church after I left in July of 1989 to assume the duties of Pastor at The First Freewill Baptist Church of Smithfield, RI, known as The Greenville Baptist Church.

Because two different churches of two different denominations were involved in my ordination, we shared the day. Since I was the Installed Pastor at the Pendleton Hill Church, the prayers and laying on of hands took place there. The church was too small for a large reception and it was only right and proper that we should also celebrate at the Congregational Church. After all, they had supported me throughout the seminary journey. Hewitt Hall, of the Congregational Church, was beautifully decorated. The women of the church presented a "Silver Tea." Helen Clark of the Congregational Church and Nelda Fox of the Pendleton Hill Church, served. It was all very formal and proper, and quite beautiful.

After all the festivities, my family and I retired to the A-frame home on Greenhaven Road. During the ride home I overheard my Dad and Uncle Marvin making comments as to what kind of beverages they might expect at the new Reverend's home . . . probably nothing stronger than tea. Everyone was surprised when they entered the kitchen and found a full bar. All was well. The Tea at the church was nice they said, but they wanted something stronger!

I opened many gifts and cards. My parents gave me a porcelain eagle in full flight and an accompanying framed needlepoint piece that mother had made of Isaiah 40:41: "Those that wait upon the Lord shall renew their strength; they shall rise up like eagles." My son, Todd, age 12 had saved his money and rode his bike over to the Catholic Bookstore in Westerly, RI to pick out a present. He was very proud of his purchase and I loved his gift. It has always hung in whatever office I have had. My mother, on the other hand, said, when she saw the Crucifix, "Well, that will have to be returned." "No," I said, "I will not return this gift, it is too important to me." You see, in our family heritage, back to the seventeenth century, our family has been rooted in the Protestant Reformation. Let me explain further:

On my mother's side her ancestors had to flee their native France because of religious persecution and take up livelihoods in Leiden, Holland. For a brief time our ancestors left Holland and went to Manheim, Germany and then migrated back to Holland. These ancestors were part of the French Reformed Church. In other words, they were Huguenots. In 1660 our Huguenot ancestors took the same spiritual and immigration journey to America as the Pilgrims took of 1642, leaving Leiden, Holland. The Pilgrims landed in Cape Cod and Plymouth, Massachusetts. My ancestors landed in Staten Island, New York eighteen years later. My Mother had deeply rooted Protestant genes, and a crucifix was just "too Catholic."

On my father's side, his ancestors were Scotch-Irish. The Scots were Presbyterian Protestants whom the British had settled/placed in Ireland for religious and economic reasons. These transposed Scots, some who married Irish men and women but retained their Protestant ways, became known as Orangemen. Even today Ireland struggles over social and economic issues that have some roots in religious discontent. My Dad had deep Presbyterian and Methodist genes so when he made a twirling finger to the temple (the crazy sign) at my first baptism by immersion at Keutman's Pond, you can understand that his "Baptism experiences" were limited to infant baptisms. He thought the baptism he had just witnessed was a bit crazy. Neither of my parents was sure about my becoming a "Baptist"; they were far more comfortable with my ordination to the Ministry of Word and Sacrament with the Congregationalists.

My Ecumenical Ordination closed the journey of discerning my call, seeking a seminary education and becoming a pastor of a small country Baptist church. My Ecumenical Ordination opened the doors to thirty years (so far) of serving Christ, His Church and His Mission. Like life itself, those thirty years have been years of joys and sorrows, births and deaths, marriages and divorces, new jobs and lay offs; truly thirty years of all the diversity of life. I have had the privilege to share these years with so many wonderful fellow Christians as an ordained minister of the gospel of Jesus Christ. It has been quite a journey!

Never Try to Baptize a Cat

I borrowed this title from a Family Circus cartoon by Bill Keane. The cartoon character, Dolly, was holding a wet, struggling, very angry cat and, at the same time, saying to her mother, "I learned a big lesson: never try to baptize a cat." Dolly must have a "thing" about baptism, because in another cartoon she is holding her doll upside down over the toilet bowl saying, "I baptize you in the name of the Father, Son and into the hole you goes."

Baptism is one of my favorite subjects. The subject and focus of my Doctor in Ministry project and thesis was to develop a curriculum which could be used for young people ages twelve or thirteen as they prepared for Confirmation or Believer's Baptism. In many of the Christian denominations young people in their pre-teen and early teen age years are encouraged to consider taking Confirmation or Baptismal vows as their own decision to follow Jesus and his teachings. Some refer to this time as "preparing to join the church." But this decision to be confirmed or baptized is far more than "joining" another organization. I would explain to my discipleship classes the idea of committing one's life to Christ, His church and His mission by using these types of ideas:

> When you are going to be a fan for the Yankees or the Red Sox teams, you have made a decision, a commitment, to that team. No one insisted that you be a loyal fan. And even if someone did insist, you could always say, "No, I want to be a Braves' fan," or even say, "Hey, I don't want to be a fan of a baseball team or a football team, I want to be a fan of hockey." Now that you are old enough to make up your own mind about following Jesus, learning to love God, to love your neighbor and learn more

> about yourself, you are being given the opportunity to decide if this is the right time for you to be baptized or to confirm the baptismal vows taken for you by your parents. The question is: Do you want to be a Christian and a Member of Christ's Church? After spending time together as a class, reading and learning about the traditions of your faith you will be given an opportunity to make a free decision to follow Jesus. Jesus does not force anyone to follow Him. Jesus invites you to be his follower. Only YOU can decide.

I designed the curriculum for children in the Baptist tradition as well as for those children who had been baptized as infants. In their tradition the next step in faith formation is called Confirmation. I called the curriculum *The Sneaker Seekers*, as sneakers are the most common footwear for this particular age group who are seeking to learn more about their faith during their faith journey. Most 12 and 13 year olds would be wearing sneakers as they took their journey of faith.

My curriculum was tested at the Chepachet Union Church, a federated church of two different denominations, the United Church of Christ and the American Baptist Church. It was also tested at The Greenville Baptist Church where I was pastor from 1989-2001. The youth group from Chepachet Union was made up of students from the United Church of Christ tradition which offers infant baptism and youngsters from the American Baptist families in the church who practiced "Believer's Baptism" also known as Adult Baptism or baptism by immersion. I purposely designed a youth curriculum that would work for federated churches, as well as for churches that practice Believer's Baptism. My dear friend, the late Reverend Thomas Bichan, who helped to test the material and used it regularly at Chepachet Union had urged me, on many occasions, to publish it, but I have never done so.

Remembering Tom Bichan, let me tell you a story about his party when he retired from Chepachet Union Church. I was asked to be one of the speakers. I told a story about how Tom and I always shared Believer's Baptism and Confirmation services, as a team, together at the Greenville Baptist Church. Why, you ask, was Rev. Bichan taking his baptismal and confirmands to the Greenville Baptist Church when he had a pastorate at Chepachet Union—well, because the Greenville church had a baptistery and Chepachet Union did not. We always held this joint service on Palm

Sunday evening and between the two churches the congregation was sizable.

Neither Tom nor I had fishing waders, which some Baptist pastors wear into the baptistery. Tom would dress/prepare with the guys in the parlor, and I would dress/prepare with the gals down the hall in a large class room. On one occasion after all the guys were ready, wearing their swim suits and white robes over them, there stood Tom in shirt, tie and boxer shorts and I came into the room. He made no signs of embarrassment. He simply put on his robe and said he was ready. Yes, his shirt, tie and boxers were baptized as well while the rest of us had simply worn our bathing suits under our white baptismal robes.

So I told this story to the retirement gathering and left the people at the party wondering about Tom's attire under his baptismal robe. Since I knew, I had seen and as a friend of a true Scotsman, I was not going to tell! Then the Catholic pastor, Father Eugene, spoke and ran the joke some more and then commented that he always wondered what that "big tub" was at the Greenville Church . . . it was too small for a swimming pool so it must have been a Jacuzzi and he wondered if he was allowed to go in it with Rev. Holden too?

The first time I had the privilege to take part in a Believer's Baptism, a baptism by immersion, was at the Pendleton Hill Baptist Church. My parents were in attendance and the entire congregation left the little church and walked over to the pond on the Keutman property. I was nervous. I had never performed a baptism before, let alone in a pond. I gathered up all my courage, putting on a good front as though I knew exactly what I was doing. I might add we did not have classes at Yale Divinity School on how to perform baptisms, weddings or funerals. It was assumed (Heaven help me) that we would learn these various services and rituals when we did our student internships. Baptism by immersion was all new to me! I grew up a Methodist where infants were baptized. My "home" church was the North Stonington Congregational Church and infants were baptized there as well. I knew how to hold a baby. I knew nothing about being IN the water.

I screwed up my courage, turned my back to the congregation and marched into the pond. It was COLD! My Lord, I thought I was going to be frozen into one of those statues all dressed in white and pigeons would come and use my head for perching and other unspeakable purposes. But I smiled and turned my face to the shore, facing my congregation and my family. Suddenly, I wanted to yell, cry, and dare I say swear . . . something was biting my foot. There I was, the semi-frozen statue, waiting for pigeons, doing the Hokey Pokey with my right foot; then my left foot. When I had composed myself and beckoned the first baptismal candidate to join me, my robe started to balloon up and now I am thinking, "I'll look like one of those crocheted items with a doll's face and white dress that one places over a roll of spare toilet paper and her arms rest on her skirt." What a site! I learned that when you plan an outdoor Believer's Baptism, you should:

- Wear a robe with a weighted hem
- Wear beach shoes
- Try to have warm water

Other than that, the baptism went wonderfully well, and I was very pleased that I hadn't dropped the candidate or allowed him to drown. I had a feeling that somehow there was a mystery which we had just entered into and I was spiritually and emotionally exhilarated, albeit, physically frozen.

When I reached the shore a little 8 year old boy, nephew of my friend Nelda, was standing by my Dad and looked up at him and twirled his finger near his temple (the crazy sign) and you know what (?)—My Dad looked at the little boy and did the same thing! My Dad never got over that baptism. As a Methodist, he had never seen a baptism by immersion. I think most Christians have not. Believer's Baptism by immersion sets Baptists apart from many other denominations.

Anyone who has been baptized by immersion can readily answer the question, "Have you been baptized?" Baptism by immersion is a dramatic event. One might not remember the exact date, or the names of others who were in the preparatory class, and one may not remember the name of the pastor, but if one has been immersed in a sanctuary baptistery, or in a lake or ocean, or at Keutman's Pond . . . one remembers!

I have many fond memories of students over the years as they prepared for their baptism. At the Second Congregational Church of Attleboro, Massachusetts, where I served as Interim Pastor from 2004-2008, I had the privilege of baptizing many infants. If an infant started to cry I immediately handed the child to a parent and proceeded. An Infant baptism is elegant and dignified. There is nothing elegant or dignified about baptism by immersion, but for those who have made this decision as a young adult or older and who have walked through the baptismal waters, it is an unforgettable experience.

Let me finish this brief essay with my most memorable time around the renewal of my baptismal vows.

My sister Martha, friends Reverend Phyllis, and Reverend Carol, and parishioners Marcia, Nelda, Jeanne and I were privileged to renew our baptismal vows in the River Jordan in February, 2000. The actual site where Jesus was supposedly baptized by John the Baptizer, is now under Jordanian control. The Israelis have arranged a place on the River banks where tourists can visit "the place where Jesus was baptized." Christians from around the world come and are baptized or they may renew their baptismal vows. My friends and I were part of a group of 42 from the Rhode Island Conference of the United Church of Christ. We spent two weeks in Israel and Jordan running where Jesus walked. When the 6 Baptists from our group decided that we wanted to renew our baptismal vows by being immersed in the waters of the Jordan, our traveling companions were stunned. What! "Isn't baptism a once in a lifetime experience?" they said. Most of our traveling companions were UCC clergy and they wanted us to explain our theology. "Why would you stand in the middle of the Jordan in a paper thin white gown over your bathing suit and be immersed? Haven't you already been baptized?" This is what we said: "We are reenacting, symbolically taking, the steps where Jesus walked. We are renewing our baptismal vows, just as some couples renew their wedding vows." It was a very moving experience. We had no idea that our companions were singing on the shore and that their numbers had grown to hundreds. We had become the tourist event for the day. For the 6 of us, it was a holy moment, a treasured moment, a sacred time for each of us, which can never be duplicated.

Baptism is so much more than a ritual, so much more that a sacrament or ordinance, so much more than a doctrine or a dogma. It has a soul-cleansing effect, with the promise of starting a new life with Christ. We have not been righteous as Christians, in regards to our dogmas and doctrines over baptism. Our relationships with our ecumenical Christian brothers and sisters have suffered because of it. Christians have divided themselves over the issues of baptism. Far too often in our Christian history, we separate ourselves from one another and there have been awful religious wars over issues of baptism and communion, also known as

The Eucharist or The Lord's Supper. There are more churches, not from addition or multiplication, but from division. Baptism, as is the Eucharist, is the very gift of God's love. That divine love cuts through the barriers we make in our human relationships; that divine love binds us together with each other and with God. It is God's way of helping us to live a renewed, regenerated and righteous life. Whether one has been baptized as an infant and confirmed in later life, or one has walked through the Believer's baptismal waters—one must never, ever, forget one's baptism. Through our baptism we have been sealed with God's love; God's love has been sealed in us.

A Brief Overview of the Shifts in Baptismal Practices

The ecumenical document, *Baptism, Eucharist, and Ministry* adopted by the Faith and Order Commission of the World Council of Churches in 1982 summarizes the meaning of baptism in the New Testament as:

> "Baptism is participation in Christ's death and resurrection (Rm 6:3-5; Col 2:12); a washing away of sin (I Cor 6:11); a new birth (Jn 3:5); and enlightenment by Christ (Eph 5:14); a reclothing in Christ (Gal 3:27); a renewal by the Spirit (Titus 3:5); the experience of salvation from the flood (I Peter 3:20-21); an exodus from bondage (I Cor 10:1-2) and a liberation into a new humanity in which barriers of division whether of sex or race or social status are transcended (Gal 3:27-28; I Cor 12:13). The images are many but the reality is one."[9]

The earliest baptismal liturgies were designed for adult Christian converts. Through their complex and symbolic actions these liturgies emphasized the mystery of human transformation through the gifts of water and the Holy Spirit. The early church struggled within and among themselves over many issues; the form of conversion being one issue. In Acts 15 the question was: "Unless you are circumcised according to the custom of Moses, can you be saved?" (Acts 15:1). The Council at Jerusalem decided, after hearing arguments from Paul and Barnabas, not

[9] Baptism, Eucharist and Ministry: Faith and Order Paper No. 111 (Geneva, World Council of Churches: 1982) 2.

to burden the converted Christian gentiles with the law of circumcision, but insisted, instead, on a variety of purity laws (Acts 15:20). There were divisive issues around baptizing the dead (I Cor 15:29); baptism which did not include the Holy Spirit (Acts 8:16); and overall divisions within the church, the Corinthian Church in particular (I Cor 3:1ff).

The prototype for Christian baptism however, was Jesus' baptism in the River Jordan. Adults were urged to repent and be baptized by the Apostles and Paul. Households were baptized (Acts 16:15); thus we may assume that infants and children were also baptized in the earliest Christian days. The norm, however, would be that the earliest baptismal liturgies were designed for adult Christian converts. During the period of persecution, anyone converting to Christianity took the risk of banishment, imprisonment or death. There was a price to be paid if one decided to follow Christ.

By the time of Emperor Constantine, 314 CE, Christianity had become the established, acceptable religion of the day. In fact, non-Christians were often abducted from the streets and forcefully "baptized." This shift makes choice a moot issue. Infants and children were regularly baptized. By the early fifth century, candidates for baptism were normally infants.[10] This shift makes baptism and the practice of Christianity a matter of course versus a matter of conviction. The sign of the cross on the forehead of an infant, with a few sprinkled drops of water, marked and sealed the child into the membership of the church. The rites of Baptism and Confirmation later became two separate practices. Often there were many years' delay from the time of baptism and the time when the Bishop could "confirm" the instructed catechumen.

By the time of the Reformation of the sixteenth century, there were well established dogmas, practices and liturgies within the established Roman Church. Among the many practices, dogmas, and liturgies with which the Reformers took issue was the place of the sacraments in the worshipping community. All liturgies underwent a variety of re-formations during this time. The baptism practices were questioned and reformed as well. All Reformers desired to re-form the existing liturgies and practices of worship and replace them with rites and practices that could be found solely in the Bible, particularly the New Testament. In their criticisms of the established church, the Reformers sought to return to the New

---

10 Paul Bradshaw, Early Christian Worship (London: SPCK,1996) 33-36.

Testament church model. They wanted a return to New Testament times, made more feasible through Luther's translation of the Bible, so that the Holy Spirit could rule in the hearts of a true community of the faithful.

Although universal agreement on theological concepts and practices was lacking among the various Reformers, most of the Reformers were concerned with an apprehension of change and suffered with a general impatience about the direction it was taking. Certainly the Reformers did not agree on the issue of infant baptism or the admittance of children to the communion table prior to confirmation, nor could they agree on the theological meaning of baptism, infant or adult. Some believed, like Zwingli, that baptism was a rite of initiation. Luther and Calvin leaned heavily on baptism as a Grace from God, an eternal election, a divine citizenship received at baptism. Luther and Calvin received infants for baptism. Barth writes, "The glory of baptism among all parts of the Church's proclamation is its 'once-for-all-ness.' For Jesus Christ died once for our sins and awakened once from the dead for our justification, once for all."[11]

The Radical Reformers such as Hübmaier and Menno Simons also wanted a return to New Testament times and biblically based practices and rites. The name "Anabaptists" (re-baptizers) was at first a derogatory name used against the Radical Reformers who would not and did not baptize infants.

These Radical Reformers believed that there was no Biblical warrant for the baptism of infants and that the church of Jesus Christ should be made up only of those adults who had made a public profession of faith. Those Christians who joined in their group who had been baptized as infants were consequently "re-baptized."

Baptism is still the center of some controversy among Christians. Disputes still arise around the value of adult believer's baptism versus the value, if any, of infant baptism.

Disputes also arise as to the role and propriety of children at the communion table, the nature and importance of catechism instructions, and the theological place of the rite of confirmation. There is limited agreement among all Christians concerning the issues of baptism. Wars have been fought and much heartache has been perpetrated over religious

---

[11] Karl Barth, The Teaching of The Church Regarding Baptism (London: SCM Press, 1959) 64..

dogmas such as infant baptism versus adult baptism. The question still remains, is baptism a matter of course or a course of conviction?

Baptists cannot agree on the subject, because there are many different Baptist denominations, beliefs and practices. "Baptist" is a generic term. In order to understand "Baptist" theology about the nature and purpose of baptism, one must inquire from the individual Baptist about his/her theological stance. There is no such thing as a "Baptist" Baptismal creed.

The First Freewill Baptist Church of Smithfield (commonly known as The Greenville Baptist Church) where I was pastor from 1989-2001 had Reformed and Radically Reformed tributaries and theological streams which joined to create the "living waters" of baptism as practiced today. The official policy of the Church, paraphrased for my readers' convenience, is as follows: "Those who seek baptism must be of an age to reason and decide about participating in the rite of baptism. The rite of baptism and the ritual of the Right Hand of Fellowship (church membership) are two distinct acts."

The same theology can be said of The First Baptist Church of North Stonington (commonly known as The Pendleton Hill Church). Two of the three churches that I served as Interim Minister, i.e. The Berean Baptist Church of Harrisville, RI and The Harbor Church of Block Island, RI both practiced baptism by immersion, also known as Believer's Baptism with the understanding that those who seek baptism must be of an age to reason and decide about participating in the ritual of baptism by immersion.

Within the American Baptist Churches (ABC/USA) tradition, many churches, but not all, practice "open membership." From its beginning in 1820 Greenville Baptist Church has practiced open membership, that is, GBC has accepted into full membership those who have been baptized as infants and come to the fellowship by letter of transfer. The Freewill Baptist tradition also accepts into membership those who have no desire to be baptized because of infirmity or a psychological fear of the water. It is possible to be a full member at the Greenville Baptist Church and decide not to be baptized, immersed or otherwise. It is also possible at GBC to be "re-baptized" if the candidate does not believe in the validity of their infant baptism, or even if he or she would simply like to be re-baptized. It is also possible to be "confirmed" at GBC so long as the rite is called a public Profession of Faith.

As more and more non-baptized adults wish to join the various denominations of churches, special rites may have to be developed specifically for them. At all the American Baptist Churches I have served as Pastor or Interim Pastor, we offered baptism by total immersion to all those old enough and who were capable of making a decision to commit themselves to Christ, His church and His mission. To answer the question, "is baptism a matter of course or a course of conviction?" in the ABC/USA churches in which I have served, the answer is: a course of conviction.

Christmas Pageants Over the Years

I am one of those sappy folk that love a good Christmas Pageant. My recollection of Christmas pageants began as a child when I attended the West View Methodist Church of West View, PA. We had all of the traditional roles to be filled.

Shepherds were dressed in their father's bathrobes and some sort of towel or scarf on their heads, with staff in hand. Many times the staff was an ordinary walking stick or something like it. There were no real shepherds in West View, PA, so we didn't know what they looked like, aside from the pictures in the children's Bible or from the shepherds that came with the flannel board story about the Nativity.

Kings had lovely crowns. There were no Burger King restaurants when I was growing up; therefore, no one had a Burger King crown. We didn't call these kings "Magi" either, and of course only boys could be given these parts. There always had to be three kings. When I taught Sunday school I liked to point out that the Bible does not call the visitors from the East, "Kings." They are called "wise men" or Magi or astrologers. There is no mention of three Kings, just Wisemen bearing three gifts. In any case, as a child, I was never cast as a King or Magi or Wise Man. Too bad, because I loved their costumes which some mother made using left over velvet in rich colors, along with their beautiful crowns.

Sheep were often the nursery school children or first graders dressed in white sweat pants, white sweat shirts and they had little sheep ears to wear. Sometimes they even wore a sheep's mask. Their only speaking part was to say "bah, bah" and look cute. And in good sheep fashion, they were usually hard to manage. I've always believed that sheep do not intentionally get lost; they just nibble their way lost.

Angels were dressed in white with a gold tinsel halo. Depending on the number of students in the Sunday school class, there could be a host of angels or just Angel Gabriel.[12] Funny, only girls seemed to be picked as angels. A child asked me once during the Children's Moment why there were never any boy angels. It was then that I realized we have done a disservice to the idea of angels and their gender. Most children don't know the names of two of the most famous angels, who happen to carry masculine names: Gabriel, and Michael.[13] Michael, the archangel, is considered a warrior and guardian of the Gate to Heaven.

Today, most angels are portrayed as cherubs: little children with wings and fat little faces or as stately adult goddess-like creatures with wings. The traditional Jewish and Christian idea of the cherub is anything but a cute and chubby creature. As described in Genesis,[14] the cherubim guard the entrance to the Garden of Eden. In Ezekiel[15] and First Kings[16] the descriptions of the cherubim have 4 faces: that of man, ox, lion and eagle. These cherubim are depicted as having four conjoined wings covered with eyes and they have ox's feet. A cherub sounds very terrifying and awesome and personally, I don't want to meet a cherub, let alone a host of cherubim.

Renaissance painters have had a great influence on how "modern day" angels are portrayed, and I suspect that the chubby little cherub owes a great deal to painters such as Botticelli and others.

In the Bible we can read many passages about the Angel of the Lord, and in the book of Revelation we read about the angels of the seven churches of Asia Minor. The Church of Jesus Christ of Latter Day Saints (Mormons) has a special angel named Moroni. His golden statue, replete with trumpet, graces the highest point of the temple in Salt Lake City. But the angels with the best Biblical description are the Seraphim[17]. The

---

12 Dan. 8:16, 9:21, Luke 1:19, 1:26

13 Jude 9; Rev. 12:7

14 Genesis 3:24

15 Ezekiel 10:17-20, 28: 14-16

16 1 Kings 6: 232-28

17 Isaiah 6:1-7

Seraph has six wings: two wings covers its face, two wings covers its feet and two wings are used to fly. The Seraph's only task is to attend the throne of God.

I write all of this information to substantiate my claim that the awesomeness of these heavenly creatures has been tamed, feminized and made infantile. Yet, every Christmas pageant must have angels, and the angels would surely always be sweet and have a place in the program where the director could cast a great number of girls.

Mary is the most important part for a girl to be cast in a Christmas pageant. I have never played the part of Mary. The girl chosen was usually the prettiest and cutest little girl in the Sunday school. In West View, PA, she was probably blond with lovely blue eyes, nothing at all like the original Mary who would have had Semitic features and would have been a young teen-age girl.

Joseph. No boy seemed to want the part because he would have to hold Mary's arm and walk her down the aisle. And when you are a boy in elementary school, the last thing you want to do is hold a girl's hand or arm. Symbolically, I suppose there are few men who would want to step up to the plate and be cast as Joseph and be the earthly father of God's Son, Jesus. In the Biblical story Joseph does not get great billing. He seems almost to have a cameo walk-on part. And yet, for the sake of history, Joseph's role as father shaped Jesus' life in such a way that when Jesus was a man his most often used metaphor to explain what God was like was the word, "Father."

That is the cast of characters for the traditional Christmas Pageant.

When I was teaching science at the Thomas School for Girls in Rowayton, Connecticut I attended a Christmas Pageant set in the medieval age. Mabel Thomas, founder of the school in 1922, wrote a play based on the Christmas story with the setting in an old English castle. The cast would include the traditional pageant characters, in addition to the English King and Queen and their court that had come to see the pageant. By 1964-1966 when I was teaching at the Thomas School, the script was cast in cement as a memorial to Miss Thomas. The costumes for the participant characters in the pageant as well as the members of the court, were extravagant. Alumni came back every year just to see the production. There were Pages, Ladies and Gentlemen-in-waiting, Knights, Squires,

Clerics, Noblemen and Noble women and other roles for the pageant. There were enough parts and costumes for each student in the school to be involved, from elementary through high school. The most coveted role of all was Mary. The girl cast as Mary was always a senior with the highest grade point average, and she had to have the approval of the Head Mistress. Her personality was part of the equation.

The pageant was held at the Rowayton Congregational Church, at least during the years that I saw this production, and I had some responsibilities for its outcome. The church was decorated with traditional wreaths and greens and the backdrop of the castle was in the center of the chancel area. Candlelight was everywhere. The Ladies-in-Waiting and Pages carried flaming candles. There were candelabras on the chancel; blazing candles were high over the pews inserted in holders on the sides of the pews. The aura of the night did seem extra holy and most especially when *O Holy Night* was sung by one of the students and when we all sang *Silent Night* at the end of the program. I am so glad I have the memories of those two special years at the Thomas School for Girls.[18]

The Christmas pageant that has given me the very best story of my 30 years of ordained ministry was the pageant at The Pendleton Hill Baptist Church, North Stonington, CT. The year was 1985.

We had decided to have two pageants that Sunday afternoon. The first pageant would be cast using only the nursery school through elementary school children. The second pageant was to be performed by the Baptist Youth Fellowship (BYF) under the direction of Dick and Dotty Wingate.

During the first pageant we had the usual characters with Timmy, age 5, and Sarah, age 4, cast as Mary and Joseph. There were no spoken lines to learn. All the children had to do was come down the aisle when their part of the story was read. They were cute, the sheep got lost, the angels sang and Timmy didn't want to hold Sarah's hand!

---

[18] The school merged with Low Heywood of Stamford, CT in 1975. Today the school is part of King Low Heywood Thomas School. The Headmistress who hired me was Mrs. Katherine Opie. The last headmistress of The Thomas School was Jean Harris. She left Thomas upon the merger to become headmistress of The Madeira School in McLean, VA. She was convicted in 1980 for the murder of her ex-lover, Herman Tarnover, author of the Scarsdale Diet.

I was sitting in the back of the church and someone tapped me on the shoulders. "Rev. Holden, we forgot to bring a baby Jesus. What should we do?" It was one of the high school kids. "Never mind, I'll ask Sarah for her dolly," I whispered. So after the children were finished with their part and Sarah was sitting in her father's lap, I went over to her and whispered, "Sarah, the BYF forgot to bring a baby Jesus. May they borrow your dolly.?" "NO!" she replied. "Sarah," I pleaded, "the BYF will be very careful with your dolly, may I use it for the next play?" "NO!" she replied a little louder and a little more firmly. I was desperate and I said, "Sarah, the BYF needs a baby Jesus." And Sarah said forcefully, "NO!." And her father said, loud enough for the entire congregation to hear, "Oh, give her the damn baby Jesus."

No one who was there that night should forget that moment. I sure have not, and I have told this story at least once every Christmas season since.

The angel Gabriel, that famous pageant night, was my son Todd. He was fourteen years old, and he had grown his first mustache. There he stood on an orange crate, dressed in a white baptismal robe, gold garland for a halo and wings made from white domestic turkey feathers, his smiling face with the pencil thin mustache proclaiming to the world, "Unto you is born this day in the city of David, a Savior who is Christ the Lord." I tear up even today thinking about it. I love Christmas pageants.

Perfect Memories of a Perfect Church

I often think of the eight wonderful years when I was Pastor at The Pendleton Hill Baptist Church, and the couple that stands out in my mind the most is Dick and Dot Wingate. It was their inspiration, effort and fortitude that helped to reactivate the church after years of neglect. I arrived at the church in 1981 as Student Pastor, serving my seminary internship under the Reverend Dick Mitchell. What a dynamic duo we were. Both of us were teachers at Pine Point School, we both graduated in 1960, both of us were devoted to Christ, His Church and His mission. My guess is that Dick had been ordained prior to 1968. I had just started Yale Divinity School in 1979. It was Dick Mitchell who asked me to join him at Pendleton Hill as he awaited the possible call as Headmaster of Pine Point. He was named Headmaster in 1981 and the good folks at Pendleton Hill Church called me to be their pastor in 1982. And through all of those exciting, heady times for Rev. Mitchell and me, there stood Dick and Dot as pillars of this little, but magnificent, church high on a hill in North Stonington, CT, with their beacons of light and love to the entire community.

I really cannot say Dick and Dottie "stood" because they were always on the go. They organized the Ham and Bean Suppers and ran the gamut from buying the ingredients, peeling apples and making the crust for Dottie's famous apple pies, to slicing the ham, mixing the beans, setting up tables and chairs in the new undercroft of the church, selling tickets, buying their own tickets and after the meal, if there were leftovers, buying the leftovers as well.

I recall one of the first Ham and Bean suppers that was put on while I worked as Pastor. There I was, like all the women, wearing my apron, hustling between tables, bringing wonderful food to the customers. One man stopped me and said, "Honey, I'd like some more corn bread," to which I replied that I would be delighted to get him more corn bread. Later he said, "Honey, I'd like some more coleslaw." No problem, I'd be glad to get him more coleslaw. The next time I passed his seat he asked for more ham and then another time he wanted more beans and so it went all evening and each time he would address me as "Honey." The last encounter went something like this: "Honey, I'd like another piece of pie," and I swear he was about to pat my bottom. Then he said, "Who is the pastor of this place now?" and I replied, "This Honey is."

Dick and Dot were sterling examples of youth leaders. Both of my youngsters had them for Baptist Youth Fellowship and adored them! No matter how busy this couple was they always had time for the youth of the church. They took the church youth group camping and skiing, water rafting and also to a national youth gathering in Estes Park, Colorado. I cannot say that my two children, Todd and Becky, thought that the best activity was cleaning the Wingate chicken coops, but somehow, Dot and Dick had the entire youth group preparing the chicken coops for a new load of chickens and they did it! I was not able to have them clean their rooms and here Dot and Dick had them shoveling chicken mature and hosing down the walls. I believe that Dot and Dick were somehow "inspired" as well as "Inspirational." Amazing.

Dick and Dot were so busy with their church work, their farm chores, civil responsibilities of Eastern Star and Masons, and of course their class room duties as teachers, as well as exemplarily parents of four active children, that I coined the verb, "Wingating." To Wingate is to be so thoroughly active, enthusiastically involved in living, loving and learning that there is no time for despondency or depression.

There were other folk at Pendleton Hill Church who were equally devoted to Christ, His Church and His mission, and they too were "Wingating." I think of Nelda Fox (later Nardone) and her family and her extended family. Whenever Nelda's sister, Linda was in town from Texas, Linda would play the piano and offer a night called "An Old Fashioned Hymn Sing." Linda's husband, Nick, often brought along his bag pipes and in full Scottish regalia would entertain the congregation, the fields, the cattle and all living things within the sound of those haunting pipes as he played "Amazing Grace." When Nelda met Charlie, he too became involved in the life of the little community and we all "Wingated," that is we never stopped living, laughing and loving. It wasn't too far into

Nelda's courtship with Charlie that she brought him to church. Nelda had been a widow, and she knew if this perfect little community of faith didn't like the one she might bring around then he would be doomed. He was accepted and loved. Once as he was leaving the worship service and I was shaking hands with the folks out the door, he gave me a huge bear hug and he DID pat me on the bottom. What male pastor can brag about something like that? And there were so many others I recall with the deepest of love: Heather LeBow, the Keutmans, the Woods, the Mitchells, the Mercers, the Medrzychowskis, the Coons and the Roachs, just a few of the names that I see in the "mirror of my mind" as I think of those early days of my first pastorate. I hold these dear folk in my heart with my deepest appreciation, admiration and affection. Is there such a thing as a perfect church fellowship? Yes! From 1981-1989 those years at Pendleton Hill Baptist Church are perfect memories of a perfect church for me!

Miracle or Misdiagnosis Either/Or Lessons Learned

For ten years I lived with the fear, strain, worry and concern that come with a diagnosis of having Multiple Sclerosis. In the early summer of 1989, after experiencing some symptoms which had given me great concern, I met Dr. Culp at the Leahy Clinic in Massachusetts. After examining me with the famous pin test and then scheduling me for an MRI scan (which was not available in 1979 when I was originally diagnosed with MS), Dr. Culp read the MRI Scan results and told me that the scan and examination showed no signs of the disease. Dr. Culp said something like this:

> "Reverend Holden, I find no signs of damage to the myelin sheaths surrounding the nerves, no plaque build up on the spinal chord or in the brain: but we can't be sure of plaque until a brain autopsy is done . . . . we don't want that now do we? If your body had some nerve damage years ago, your nervous system has adjusted and compensated for that damage. I have read your earlier medical reports. I will not dispute them. MS is a funny disease. It can show symptoms in one major episode and you may never have another episode. Maybe that is what has happened. Maybe not. Who is to say? What I can tell you is that I find no evidence to support such a diagnosis today."

Needless to say, I was overwhelmed with joy. What I did not expect from Dr. Culp was his next question which seemed to come out of the clear blue. "Reverend Holden, when are you going to find yourself a larger church?"

That question really threw me. We had never talked about the Pendleton Hill Church. We had never talked about any "church" period! We had spent all of our time going over medical history, lab reports, x-rays and MRI scans. How did Dr. Culp know I was serving a small rural church? How did Dr. Culp know I was thinking about finding a larger church with a larger salary to help support my children?

I've learned over the years that God sometimes sends us messengers—angels, if you will. Dr. Culp was an angel, a messenger from God. Oh, Dr. Culp was not a celestial spiritual being, some heavenly vision or other deified messenger, but he was an angel because he carried a message to me. Within several months of my visit to the Leahy Clinic where I had met with Dr. Culp I was called to be the Senior Pastor of the First Freewill Baptist Church of Smithfield, commonly known as the Greenville Baptist Church. I have learned to look for angels who carry divine messages. God uses ordinary men, women and children to be divine messengers. Unfortunately, you cannot expect such an occurrence. When it happens, you will know it.

Miracle or misdiagnosis? Does it have to be an either/or situation? I do believe in miracles! I can relate to the miracle of the hemorrhaging woman in the Bible.[19]

I learned so much about living with a disability during those ten years.

When I was told I had Multiple Sclerosis I began to read everything I could find on the subject. There was no internet to surf in those days. There were no blogs, twitter, Facebook or chat rooms from which I might gather information. I had the Westerly Library and the MS Society literature. I recall the day a nurse from the MS Society arrived at my home to interview me and to tell me how the MS Society might be of help to me. I told her what my doctor had said, "Stay away from any support groups. You will only become depressed." This woman intuitively knew that it would be best for me to learn about the disease through my own research. She was very helpful in signing me up for the monthly newsletter and sending me packets of information. She would periodically phone

[19] Kings James Bible. Luke 8: 43-48 "And a woman having a issue of blood twelve years, which had spent all her living upon physicians, neither could be healed of any, came behind him and touched the border of his garment: and immediately her issue of blood stanched."

and ask how I was doing. She was there to help and not condemn. I was extremely appreciative because, at the time, she was my lifeline to hope.

It is unfortunate that there are some Christians, not all, by any means, who will condemn a person just when that person needs the most help. I am thinking of the "good" Reverend from Westerly who said that God was punishing me because I was attempting to enter the ordained ministry. During that time when I needed friends to comfort me, encourage me and help bear the burden, I received criticism and a heavier burden from a Christian. He was just adding another rock to the pile.

I have learned that one of the biggest travesties against "grace" is to heap guilt on top of agony. Because some church clergy have not always been equipped to deal with suffering, they have, instead, not always offered compassion in someone's time of need: the church has often offered blame. Instead of obeying God's command to lift the heavy burdens, God's own people often increase the burden without any thought of compassion. So many Christians repeat the mistakes that Job's friends made, each friend insisting that somehow Job had caused his own suffering.[20]

I like Eugene Peterson's translation of 2 Corinthians 1: 4: "God comes alongside us when we go through hard times, and before you know it, he (God) brings us alongside someone else who is going through worse times so that we can be there for that person just as God was there for us."[21]

I think that compassion is my principal learning. God gives to us so that we can give to others. God comforts us so that we can comfort others. God encourages us so that we can encourage others. God advocates for us so that we can advocate for others. God stands by us so that we can stand by others. The Christian life is about loving, giving, caring, comforting. Jesus' ministry was centered on helping people who were hurting, and when He saw people in discomfort and pain, He was quick to discern their hurts and helplessness and apply a remedy or a word of comfort.

---

20 Job's three friends, Eliphaz, Bildad, and Zophar sat with Job for seven nights and seven days and no one spoke a word for they saw that Job's suffering was very great. But then when they did try to offer words of comfort, their words were of condemnation: Job had sinned, Job must repent, Job's guilt deserves punishment.

21 Eugene Peterson. The Message. The Bible in Contemporary Language. Navpress, Colorado Springs, Co. 1993.

I learned during the earliest months of my condition that the natural and real world is not hospitable to people who cannot negotiate stairs. There are architectural physical barriers everywhere and especially at YDS. I used a cane. The first cane I bought was black with a solid brass handle in the shape of a duck's head. It was very heavy, too heavy in fact. If you were to look under the duck's head you will see I had it engraved with my social security number. I could never remember my number and it seemed I needed to know this number every time I turned around at Yale. Since that first cane, I have acquired several others, most of them much lighter to carry. My Dad gave me a cane that folds, with a pistol grip for the handle. It is very handy to use when traveling. Mark Wingate made me a cane holder, like an umbrella rack, which I used at the house on Greenhaven Road and which I took with me and used at Barnes Street in Greenville, RI. Church members, from the Pendleton Hill church gave me a cane from Africa with an elaborately carved handle and staff. I had decided early on, that if I did need a cane, I would never use an ugly cane. All of my canes are quite beautiful and a few are very sophisticated. The ugly ones got trashed.

My years of commuting to YDS, wrestling with the academic rigors of intellectual life, and juggling home life chores and responsibilities, were exciting and nourishing years. Even after my husband's departure and the added stress of finances and single parenthood, I recall those years at YDS with the greatest of fondness. If my body wasn't at top speed, my mind certainly was. God compensates! I learned a great deal about myself: that I was capable of high caliber academic work and that I could compete on a level I never dreamt possible.

I've learned not to question why things happen that can, and often do, cause people pain and suffering. I can't answer the question "why." I ask the questions: "How can I help? How can I show that I care? How can I support you in this crisis? What can I give?" I refuse to have or accept a theology that envisions a God who randomly terrorizes people with natural disasters, accidents, disease, disappointment, depression and death. Rather, my theology is based on a loving God who cares, who loves, who supports, who walks with and through these crises with us.

I've learned that people need people, and we need one another even more in times of difficulty. We need to reach out and touch one another in some meaningful way when trouble comes. People, especially those under stress, don't need judgment and criticism, faultfinding and finger-pointing in difficult times. These judgments only make the burdens heavier. Everyone needs compassion. During the difficult times we need friends to comfort us, encourage us and help us bear the burden. For me, I have found that the sharing of joys and of sorrows, the carrying of burdens and the celebrating of victories have best been done in the Body of Christ known as the church, so long as that church is spiritually connected to God and is a healthy place. For me, when the local church is healthy, the local church is the best place to find wholeness and peace in the midst of chaos and troubles.

Unfortunately, there are too many troubled churches in the world, and they have lost their ability to be the sanctuaries of healing and grace. Some churches, today, are lost in their own distractions, often caused by their own misdeeds or ignorance, and are unable to extract themselves from their world problems, and therefore are, in a sense, dysfunctional.

My entire ordained ministry has been devoted to helping to make the local church a place of healing, hope and love. I have not always been successful, but I persist in trying, and I have learned that the final harvest is God's, not mine.

The Call to Greenville

The year was 1989 and I had been pastor of the Pendleton Hill Baptist Church since 1981.

In the December 24th mail, along with all the Christmas cards and other greetings, came an inquiry, addressed to me, from the search committee of the Greenville Baptist Church in Greenville, RI. Dear Reader, you must remember that Christmas and Easter are the two busiest times of the year for any cleric. I was frantically working to get ready for the Christmas Eve service at the Pendleton Hill Church in North Stonington, CT, so I ignored the letter until early January. Although I say that I ignored the letter, I must admit that the subject matter of the letter hardly left my subconscious mind. After the holidays were over and all the cleaning up had been accomplished, I called the chair, Ruth, and we talked for a while and eventually set up an appointment date when I would go up and visit with the search committee.

I was very happy at the Pendleton Hill church, and this invitation truly came out of the blue. Pendleton Hill was the place where I did my student internship under the tutelage of my friend the Reverend Richard "Dick" Mitchell. This was the congregation that led me to ordination, along with the North Stonington Congregational Church. I loved the charm and simplicity of the buildings and the unpretentious way of life of the rural congregation. The original congregation that eventually organized as the Pendleton Hill First Baptist Church was "gathered" in 1743, and it became the second oldest Baptist church in Connecticut, following the "gathering" of the Old Mystic Baptist Church which was the oldest Baptist church. The Pendleton Hill Church building was postcard perfect: a little white clapboard structure with a high steeple sitting at the peak of Pendleton Hill on a small knoll surrounded by farm lands and behind it, the church cemetery. There was a one-room schoolhouse on the property as well as two outhouses, each replete with the traditional slice of moon carved in the doors. I liked to brag when I went to denominational meetings that I had four buildings to supervise. Clergy are better at bragging than fishermen!

The people of faith at this little country church were committed to Christ, His church and His mission. The Wingates, whom I have mentioned before, were the backbone of the church and the youth group. We had the Foxes, the Mercers, the Keutmans, the Lebows, the Millers, the Mitchells, the Woods, and several other families who worked hard to maintain this historic structure and who grew spiritually in this special place. This was the group of people who held me and my children in prayer as I was going through my divorce. This was the group of people, along with the friends at North Stonington Congregational Church who prayed and financially supported my years at Yale Divinity School. This was the group of people who put on the famous Ham and Bean suppers every other month and the extraordinary Chicken Barbeque each summer. This was the group of people who nurtured my children during their formative years, right through their teen age years. The Youth Group, and the Summer Camp provided by the Church were excellent learning experiences for my children. I loved everything about Pendleton Hill Baptist Church: the people, the buildings, the excitement of one's first job. I didn't want to leave and yet I knew I had to find a larger parish with a larger financial "package" that would help me send my children to college. I was pastor at the Pendleton Hill Church for eight wonderful years: 1981-1989.

With mixed emotions that I cannot possibly describe, I replied to the Greenville Baptist Church search committee. They had been looking for a settled pastor for over three years. They loved their interim pastor and his wife, and they obviously were not in any great hurry to find a settled pastor. They had experienced several set-backs in their search, and several potential candidates had backed out. In truth, the Greenville Baptist Church had a terrible reputation within the state of Rhode Island American Baptists as a place that was very hard on their pastors. The longest pastorate was with Dr. White, and he stayed for 14 years, resigning to join the navy in 1942. But many of the pastorates were less than 5 years. I, of course, at that time knew nothing about the Greenville Baptist Church nor their reputation. They had sent me their profile and I courteously replied. As fate would have it (actually I believe it was in God's design), I met with the search committee several times, and they asked me to "Preach for Call" on May 23, 1989. To Preach for Call is when the congregation has a time to meet the candidate the search committee has selected, and after several arranged "meet and greet" opportunities and after the candidate leads the congregation in worship and preaches, the congregation votes on the search committee's candidate.

I remember I wore a cream skirt and a beautiful "Jones of New York" beige and cream jacket. Todd was a senior at Ledyard High School, at the time, and Becky was finishing her sophomore year at Stonington High School. They had mixed emotions (along with yours truly) about this move, if the vote was affirmative. Todd would be going off to Unity College in Maine so a move to Greenville would not be as traumatic as it would be for Becky who was happy and settled at Stonington High and one of their star athletes.

My children were not happy about my professional desires, but they understood why I needed to find a larger church. It was financial, of course, but it was also a way for me to broaden my experiences as a pastor. I had spent some of my time during the previous four years as an Area Minister for the American Baptist Churches of Connecticut which I enjoyed. But with that part time job and the "full" time position at Pendleton Hill, I still was not in the financial place I needed to be at the age of 47 with two children to help educate. There was no such thing as a "savings account" and we just managed. I knew I needed to have a better income not only for my own needs but also for long-range plans.

The congregational vote was favorable and I was no longer "the candidate" now I was the "called pastor" of the First Freewill Baptist Church of Smithfield, more commonly known as the Greenville Baptist Church. I began my ministry August 1, 1989. I ended my ministry at Greenville on May 31, 2001, roughly 12 years. My ministry was the second longest pastorate at Greenville and their first woman as settled pastor. During those twelve years of ministry, there were ups and downs as anyone has in her career. The congregation grew numerically as did the Sunday school. The congregation also grew in their mission outreach. There were many wonderful Christian members of the church, but some of the old devilish ways, attitudes and behaviors were never truly exorcized and I knew when I resigned, that the health of the congregation was still poor. I had given this congregation my very best service, and I worked very hard for its spiritual health as well as its fellowship health. Some patients resist all efforts and never get better. Some churches have an embedded dysfunction and, therefore, fellowship, missions, educational and spiritual health will always elude them. Greenville was one such place. When I resigned I had no idea what I would do or where I would serve, if ever again. However, all things considered, had I not resigned I would not be able to rejoice in my new "calling" of Interim Ministry. But that is another story and other chapters.

While I served as pastor at Greenville Baptist, I was very active in the American Baptist Churches of Rhode Island, serving for seven years as the chair of the Standing Committee on Ordained Ministry. There are over twenty people who were ordained in Rhode Island who have my signature on their ordination certificate: i.e., 20 clergy whom I helped to shepherd through the often exasperating ordination process.

My daughter, Becky, was able to adjust readily to life in Greenville, RI. When she and I first came to Greenville, we had to live several months in the church parsonage while I negotiated the sale of our home in Pawcatuck and the purchase of the new home on Barnes Street in Greenville.

The Greenville parsonage, an 1880's Federal Style house, had been neglected both externally and internally and had not had a family living in it for over 5 years. I am sure that Becky still has memories of when Sue, a member of the search committee, took her through the parsonage while I was tied up in a meeting with the rest of the search committee. Becky said to me in the car as we were driving back home to Pawcatuck, "I'm not living in that shitbox." I said, "Why not? I didn't get a chance to see it, tell me about it." "You wouldn't believe it if I did told you. The rooms have this god-awful wall paper everywhere; some of the paper has fuzzy patterns; the third floor rooms are done with soldiers and 'Where is Waldo' paper; and the kitchen is so bright yellow that you need sunglasses to look at it. There is smelly old shag carpet everywhere. I won't live there!"

We did live there for several months. It was a scream! When people from Pawcatuck and Stonington came to visit us, I would meet them in the kitchen with my empty coffee can and told them that for a donation of a quarter, which would go to missions, I would take them on a tour of the place. We made money for missions and all had a good laugh. Becky was right! There WAS flocked paper in the living room-dining room in hideous brown. Flocked paper was also in the master bedroom in screaming red which reminded me of the house of ill repute in an old John Wayne movie. There was blue flocked paper in the room Becky would claim as her bedroom and brown striped paper in the third bedroom on the second floor. The third floor had three bedrooms and a bath decorated for small boys, a soldier theme in one room, a circus theme in another, a farmland in the third room and "Where is Waldo" in the bathroom. One of the first floor rooms that I claimed for my office was papered with stained patriotic eagles which I assume are still there. I placed bookcases and large pictures over the worse of the stains. There were fireplaces in most of the first and second floor rooms. This historic house needed a great deal of work and the search committee had made it clear that they did not want me (or anyone else) to live there. Offices would be a fine use, but they would give me a housing allowance toward my own home. We knew our stay at the parsonage was temporary, and it was a great celebration when Becky and I moved in October to our new home on Barnes Street.

By October, 1989, Becky was already the elected captain of the high school tennis team. She was making friends at the Smithfield High School. Her girlfriends from Stonington still came to visit her, and she had a car which made it possible for her to drive back to Stonington whenever she wished. Todd was settled as a freshman at Unity College. I was pastor of a decent sized congregation with adequate facilities for the thriving Sunday school of 100 students and a sanctuary and fellowship space sufficient to accommodate the congregation of over 250 folk. I began, and finished, my doctoral work while at Greenville. I was able to afford to send both of my children to college, Todd to Unity College and Becky to the University of Connecticut. Their father and I shared the expenses equally. I was able to uphold my share. I am proud of that accomplishment.

As I look back over those years as pastor of the Greenville Baptist Church, I am pleased with the service I gave and the creativity and spirituality that I offered in worship. As I look in the "mirror of my mind", I see with fond memories my teaching ministry: the many adult opportunities offered those 12 years; my 6th grade Sunday school classes; and the annual baptism classes. During those years I honed my preaching skills and spent several years preaching without notes or a manuscript as a way to spontaneously bring the spoken word alive. My aging short term memory no longer allows me to preach that way today. Today, I spend a great deal of time thinking about the here after. I walk into a room and say, "What am I here after?" I loved being the pastor of the Greenville Baptist Church and the people of God of worshipped and served with me there.

I am pleased as I recall and reflect upon our first mission trip to the Dominican Republic and what we learned from the mission trip to Dungannon, VA. I have no regrets about my ministry at Greenville Baptist, with one exception. My only regret is that I felt compelled to resign after almost 12 years of ministry when I realized that I could no longer make significant changes to the overall spiritual health of the congregation. For my own spiritual and mental health and for the sake of my family, I realized I had to resign. My battle scars are as intense as my wounds from a broken marriage. These two periods of my life have shaped me, both in spirit and character, as well as in freedom. I've known the peaks and valleys of the joy and sorrow in marriage as well as in the pastorate at Greenville. These experiences made me who I am today, so I need to claim them and learn from them. As Henri Nouwen, one of my professors at Yale Divinity School, wrote: We are the "wounded healers" and "Jesus is God's wounded healer." As I meditated on the wounded-ness of Jesus and how he was and is the source of life for others, I concluded that as a disciple of Jesus I can not expect to live life without pain, but through pain I can become a source of life for others as well.

Henri Nouwen wrote in his book *The Wounded Healer*, "When we become aware that we do not have to escape our pains, but that we can mobilize them into a common search for life, those very pains are transformed from expressions of despair into signs of hope."[22]

Only after the pain of leaving Greenville was I able to come to terms with my ministry there and to acknowledge and rejoice in the new signs of hope of doing Interim Ministry. This acknowledgment and joy did not happen overnight! I spent a year meditating, weeping, praying and traveling in the proverbial "wilderness." It was my friend the Reverend Tom Bichan and the good folk at the Berean Baptist Church in Harrisville, RI who prevailed upon me to return to the active ministry in the role as Interim Pastor. This role has been an exciting chapter in my life.

---

22 Henri J. M. Nouwen, *The Wounded Healer*(Garden City, NY Image Books), 93.

Celebrating my 50th Birthday 1992

Funny Things That Have Happened on the Way to the Office

I was running late for the funeral. I had a problem with my well aged and aging car. It was making a very loud knocking/banging sound under the hood, and I had to make it another 8 miles or so up Route 2 to the Pendleton Hill Church. As I left River Road in Pawcatuck and went under the bridge onto Route One, there on the corner was a gas station. It may have been a Mobil Station, I'm not sure. In any case, I pulled in, jumped out of my car and hurried in and asked the very young attendant if he could look under my hood and see if he could discover the reason for the noise. What I actually said was, "Good morning. I'm Reverend Holden and I am on my way to conduct a funeral and I am having trouble with my car." And he sarcastically said, "Yah, well I'm the Queen Mother." And, then I said, without missing a beat, "How do you do your majesty. Will you kindly look to my car?"

Women in ministry receive very little respect as a cleric. At least this woman didn't, especially not in a Catholic state like Rhode Island. I have been denied the usual clerical visiting privileges in hospitals, simply because I don't "look like a minister." When that occurred, I usually went to the administrator's office, showed him my business card, and insisted that the nurse on duty be alerted that I would be on the floor. Some Protestant clergy women, as well as women Episcopal priests, have started wearing clerical collars. I tried that once. I took one look at myself in the mirror and jumped two feet, all the while saying two hail Marys. I haven't worn a clerical collar since—it is not my style.

One day while visiting the Fatima Hospital in North Providence, I was wearing a skirt in the Black Watch tartan plaid pattern (black, blues and greens), with a white blouse and navy blue blazer. The doorman greeted me with, "Good morning, Sister." I stopped wearing that outfit as well, although the few times that I did wear it, I had less difficulty getting in to see patients with that outfit. Sister—Indeed! So many times throughout my travels with Phyllis, we have been asked the question: "You both look alike. Are you sisters?" Our stock answer has become, "No, we're Protestants."

I was in my office at the Greenville Baptist Church, going through my usual routine of opening mail, and other daily work, and in came a woman full of rage. She was waving a copy of *Time* magazine and she shouted, "Have you seen this article about Jesus?" It so happened that I had. In fact *Newsweek* had also written a similar article about the "Jesus Seminar." From my understanding, the "Jesus Seminar" consisted of various scholars, who by consensus, reported on the historical authenticity of the sayings and events surrounding Jesus' life. Both *Time* and *Newsweek* were reporting on the "Jesus Seminar" results during the Easter week and each magazine had a picture of Jesus on the cover.

I said to the gal, "Sit down and we'll talk. Tell me what makes you so upset about the article," figuring she would be concerned because one of her favorite Jesus quotations was being "attacked" as non-authentic. I was very wrong. She sat, waving her magazine and sputtered, "I'll tell you what is wrong: this picture doesn't even look like Jesus." The cover didn't look like her treasured image of Jesus that so many love, that is: Sallman's, "Head of Christ" with his blue eyes and wavy light brown hair with golden highlights. Now, whenever someone comes to me upset about some expectation or personal preference which has not been met, I say quietly to myself, "And he doesn't even look like Jesus."

The first funeral that I conducted at the Greenville Baptist Church was from the funeral home up the road from the church. It has since changed hands and name, but the name is not important. After all the people in attendance had been excused to their cars, which were lined up in the middle of Route 44, the elderly funeral director who was standing next to the casket said to me, "Come over here." I went over to the casket. He opened both sections of the casket cover and said, "Look!" I looked and all I saw was a deceased lady, properly dressed with her pearls. "Well," he said, "do you see?" "See what?" I said. "Do you see she has on her shoes?" "Yes, I see she has on her shoes." "Well, I just wanted you to know that when I do my job people are properly dressed and that includes their shoes. Some funeral guys don't. So you remember, if they come from here they'll have on their shoes. I cover all details myself! I'm running a quality place." "Yes, I'll remember."

We finally had all the flowers and the casket loaded into the hearse and off we drove to the cemetery. I said I would ride along in the hearse because I had no idea where we were going in North Scituate, because I was new to the area. When we got to the ancient cemetery in the center of the town of North Scituate, the hearse was too big for the curve on the cemetery road and it got stuck! In the process of getting the hearse unstuck, the finish on the hearse got badly scratched. Now the driver was in a foul mood. We arrived at the grave site to discover there was no grave liner: just a big hole with mounds of dirt on the side. There was no artificial grass to pretend we were somewhere else; there was nothing to hide the stark reality of death. The funeral director tried to explain to the family that we could not bury their beloved until the grave liner arrived. Now we were all standing around in 90 degree heat with at least 70 percent humidity. The family decided we should proceed with the graveside service, even though there would be no "burial" at this time. We "proceeded" and we left with "Grandmother" still in her casket, the casket leaning precariously on its side on this mound of dirt, but at least we knew that she had on her shoes.

I went back to the funeral home with a different driver in a different car. On the entire trip back to the funeral home, this driver went on and on about how he had never seen such a thing and he knew that the "old man," referring to the director, would be furious. Someone had goofed. Our waiting around had delayed this driver and he was anxious to get to his next appointment. I thanked the driver for bringing me back to the funeral home, explained once again, that I had only been in town 24 hours, so I appreciated this lift. I went to get my pocketbook and it was not there. I suddenly remembered that in the excitement of the bare, unlined crater, I had left my handbag in the hearse. So were my car keys. I had only one thing I could do, I asked this harried driver if he would kindly take me back to the hearse so I could get my handbag and my car keys. Let me just say he did, but he was one very unhappy "camper"!!!.

When we arrived back to the cemetery, there sat the "old man" in his shirt sleeves, sitting on the mound of dirt, next to the casket, with perspiration dripping from his face . . . waiting. It looked as if the casket had slipped a little toward that open grave but had fortunately stopped, so now it was more than precariously perched: the casket rested half on the mound of dirt and half over the grave. It was a memorable sight and a memorable funeral! I have never left my car keys in a hearse since!

Rebecca and Todd 1993

Words of Love

I've never forgotten his romantic overture, his expression of love and his offering of gifts. When he came to the house unannounced and declared his love, I was not the only one surprised! Phyllis was overwhelmed with his intense desires. She had been doing her counted cross stitch and when she heard his declaration of devotion, she stabbed herself and bled all over the cross stitch canvas.

I don't remember his name, although his wife's name was Lynn but he always called her, "The Redhead." He was one of the many sextons the Greenville Baptist Church had hired over the 12 years I was pastor. These janitors came and went. Many often had emotional and or addiction problems, so they didn't stay very long. This man would prove to be no exception.

I had called in sick on that particular day, infamous in my memory. I shall never forget it. I called my Dad and told him how the sexton spoke to me of his love and Dad just roared and said, "I don't think that line would have ever won over your mother." I don't think I was too ill, as I recall, but enough to make me stay at home for that day.

Sometime after we had had dinner and we were settled into watching the evening news, a knock was heard at the door. Since we were rarely home for an evening we thought this most odd, as did the dog, Honey. She roused her old arthritic bones incredibly fast and welcomed the opportunity to practice her protective bark.

I settled the dog, opened the door and there stood the sexton, holding a bouquet of red roses, a bottle of burgundy, and a limp bag of shrimp. I wasn't much in the mood for entertaining, especially this person, at that hour, especially when he was supposed to be at work. What could I do? I had to be polite and invite him in as the area of the stoop and the front door was very narrow and there wasn't room for me, the dog and the man in that tight space.

In he came, grinning, holding out his gifts to me as he weaved into the hallway wall. The whiskey vapors escaped off his breath like the early morning mist rising off Lake Loch Ness. "Are you ok?" he stammered. "I've been so worried when I heard you were sick, I just had to come over and make sure you are OK."

"I am fine, really: just a nuisance cold or virus. I expect I'll be back to work tomorrow," I said, trying to figure out how to get him to go home and not back to the church in his condition.

"But you don't understand," he slurred. "I rushed right out of work to get you these," as he pushed the roses, wine and shrimp into my hands. "I am really worried," he said or something to that effect, I, not hearing all his words which came out raw and fuzzy.

"Thank you very much. You are very kind, but I will see you at work tomorrow. Now please head home tonight, I don't think you need to return to the church . . . just go straight home." I was not about to suggest that I drive this poor inebriated soul home, I simply wanted him out of my house. I was very thankful that I was not alone in the house.

And then he lurched toward me, got his face into mine and said the most memorable and remarkable declaration of love I have ever received . . .

"If it weren't for the Redhead, I'd be all over you like flies on a turd."

A Bible Study Surprise

Ethel Stickney's Bible study class had been meeting for years, and it consisted of all women. These women had shared stories of raising children, losing their husbands, and now as elderly widows, they shared their joys and concerns about aging. When I came to Greenville Baptist Church there were 6 elegant and distinguished women in the group. Each woman was very active in the church, some of them holding church offices.

Ethel's class met next door to my office for the 12 years I was pastor. They always met on Thursday, and then they went over to the Kountry Kitchen Restaurant for lunch after class.

So the day was Thursday. There was spring in the air, the Irises were just beginning to bloom, and the women arrived dressed in their Spring finery. One by one, they came through the back kitchen door: Marion, Fran, Peg, Ethel, Kathy and Eleanor, my favorite mentors. Most were in their 80s, except for Eleanor who was only in her 60s. I always had coffee ready for them, and we carried on easy conversation until Ethel was ready to begin her class. I greeted them as usual. We had the usual exchange of hugs and kisses, catching up on news, and then they went to study and I went to work in my office.

When class was over we reversed the opening procedures. Coffee cups were returned to the kitchen sink, hugs and kisses were exchanged and off the women went to lunch.

This one particular, memorable, Thursday was different. When it came time to say the good-byes I noticed that Marion smelled peculiar. "Odd," I thought, "she didn't smell funny when she came in or I just hadn't noticed." Then when Fran and Peg said good-bye I thought "they smell funny too. Funky." Kathy and Eleanor were ready to depart and they just plain stunk! And so did Ethel! What in the world had happened?

I said nothing, of course, and off they went to the Kountry Kitchen as always.

I went into the study room and looked around. Nothing that I could see would give me a clue as to the reason for the odd odors. Then, from my office out bounded a little white terrier. He belonged to a church family. I was watching him while they were away on vacation and so I had brought him to the office. Click, the lights went on! The dog must have done something naughty in the study room. I began to do a more thorough investigation. Sure enough, under the table, ground into the brown and white 1960's shag rug was the remains of the dog's business. The rest was on the feet of the elegant and distinguished ladies who had just gone off to the Kountry Kitchen for lunch!

I never said a word to them. And to this day I have always wondered, "When did they discover that the bottoms on their shoes were covered in dog pooh?" Let me tell you, it was an awful job getting that mess out of the shag rug, especially when it all looked the same!

Friendship and Betrayal

I don't recall when Ivan, (not his given name), and his family first started coming to Greenville Baptist Church, but it didn't take very long before he and his entire family were my good friends. I would often walk around our neighborhood with his wife. Their children were in high school when I first met them, and I attended their graduations from high school. I eventually met the entire extended family who was from down South. I had baptized Ivan and each of his children. I recall that when it had come time for the Baptism, Ivan had broken his leg, but he insisted that the baptism not be postponed. He would wrap the cast in a garbage bag as protection from the immersion. He did and the baptism was not postponed. He was a big man, and my greatest fear was dropping him. The complication of a leg in a cast only intensified my worries, but the baptism went perfectly.

Ivan was a research scientist at one of the area's hospital and he taught advanced biological subjects at one of the local Rhode Island colleges. He once took me to his hospital office and showed me the electron microscope that he used and introduced me to so many of his colleagues. We had lots to talk about as I hold a degree in Biology, and we had many common interests. He was my best male friend at Greenville. I trusted him completely. He was a relatively new Christian and so he thirsted for spiritual knowledge. He participated in the Bible Studies offered over the years at Greenville. I taught a variety of these courses; the Associate Minister lead a course and an ordained woman who was a member of the GBC lead a wonderful course called, *Kerygma,* an intense course of Bible study.

When I was the pastor at Pendleton Hill I took the *Kerygma* course offered for 52 weeks by the pastor of the Old Mystic Baptist Church. From my own experience I know that this *Kerygma* Program was stimulating, was relevant to my life, and pulled together all of my Biblical learning's from seminary. What a great experience I had!

From the *Kerygma* web site[23] participants and leaders will:

- Learn the basics and complexities of the Bible
- Develop skills for interpreting Scripture
- Apply learning from the Bible to personal and corporate life in today's world

Ivan found these statements to be true for his life. He would often tell me during that year of *Kerygma* that the study was one of the most powerful and exciting times of his life! He also would share with me how much the leaders, especially the "Reverend," meant to his spiritual growth. He often told me how much he held the Reverend and me in high regard and how we had infused his life with new hope and spirituality.

His wife was delighted that Ivan "had found Christ." She explained and related how she had longed for years to be in a church fellowship atmosphere but for years had denied herself and acquiesced to and followed Ivan's directions that "Sundays were for family which did not include church." Once the family began coming to Greenville Baptist Church, everyone was unfailingly active. The young adults were in the youth group, Ivan's wife sang in the choir, Ivan became the Mission Chair and organized our week long mission trip to Dungannon, VA. Many times during our walks together, his wife would tell me that since her family was all so far away she was so glad she could include me in her family. Even their dog, the white terrier, got along with me, the very dog that left his pooh on the shag rug for the dear ladies to step in! It was a good friendship. It was even a great friendship and a friendship that was stimulating and enriching.

After a while, I became aware that Ivan had started to attend a Bible study at a very conservative church near town. I also knew that as a co-leader of the Greenville Baptist Church adult Sunday school, Ivan and the church Moderator, who was also the other co-leader, spent hours together, studying and preparing for their class. Their leadership skills and ideas set the tone, as well as, the theology and mind-set for the adult class. I was never concerned but confident in their abilities, and I never worried.

---

23 http://www.kerygma.com/About_us.html

The two leaders and I seemed to be on the same wave length, and as they say "reading from the same page of music," or so I thought. I did not attend any of their sessions/classes. I was teaching the 6th grade class, but I was confident of their abilities.

Ivan's attendance at the conservative church's Bible study did not worry me. Now, as I look back, it should have worried me. I was naïve! I was so trusting. I truly believed Ivan was simply soaking up as much study and spiritual nourishment as he could when he was off studying at the neighboring conservative church. He was still active at GBC. He still chaired the Mission Board. He still co-led the Adult Sunday school class, and as far as I knew—he was still my friend and I his spiritual mentor.

The theology at the conservative church was at the opposite end of the theological spectrum from mine. Somehow, Ivan became convinced that the gospel message preached at this conservative church was more in tune with his spiritual needs than those preached by me, and he also felt that the conservative teachings were certainly closer to the Biblical message his wife had grown up with in South Carolina as a devout Southern Baptist. Ivan and his family began to attend the conservative church for worship as well as for study. I missed them. I couldn't understand how an intelligent man like Ivan could get hooked into a narrow-minded, exclusive, judgmental message of salvation.

I should explain what I mean by a "conservative church." In theology there is a rather substantial difference in the way that Biblical scripture is interpreted. From the conservative church's web site that Ivan and his family chose to attend and join, the following is their stated belief on the authority of Scripture:

> "We believe that the sixty-six books of the Old and New Testaments as originally written were God-breathed, both verbally and in every part. We believe God, Who is Truth, communicated through Spirit-controlled men so that the Scriptures are without error and therefore authoritative in all they teach and in all matters they touch. We believe the Bible is the supreme revelation of God's will for men and constitutes the only infallible guide for faith and life."[24]

24 http://www.osbc.org/beliefs.html

The Greenville Baptist Church belongs to the American Baptist Churches USA. From the denomination's web site, one will read the following about how ABC churches are encouraged to interpret the Bible:

> "Our affirmation of the priesthood of all believers arises from a conviction that all who truly seek God are competent to approach God directly. We cherish the freedom Christ has granted us as individual believers and distinctive congregations. The Apostle Paul, in his letter to the church in Galatia and in other writings, emphasizes that freedom. Because of that, we have tended to avoid embracing prepared creeds or other statements that might compromise our obligation to interpret Scripture as individuals within the community of faith under the guidance of the Holy Spirit."[25]

The authority of scripture is just one of the differences between a fellowship like GBC and a more conservative fellowship. This is not a thesis on the theological differences but rather a brief look of how scripture is used within a conservative church.

One day in the winter of 2001 Ivan stopped by to visit with me in my office. I greeted him with a warm hug and kiss. I was genuinely pleased to see him! I had missed him and the entire family! I wanted to reconnect. We spoke of the family. The young people were at College and doing well, his wife was still working hard at her business, he had some concerns about a grant for his work at the college, etc. And then he dropped the shoe and said something to the effect that he and the family would be asking to have their membership transferred to the conservative church. I said I was sorry to lose them as members at GBC. He then dropped the other shoe and said, "Well, I can't have someone with your lifestyle in my pulpit."

I was floored. I said, "What lifestyle do you mean?" He said, "You know what I mean." And I said, "No I don't. I get up in the morning, walk our dog Honey, clean up after the dog, come to work, usually I'm here until after 9 p.m. and then I go home, walk the dog and go to bed. What life style do you mean?" "Well" he said, "you live with a woman."

---

25 http://www.abcusa.org/WhoWeAre/Identity/Bible/tabid/59/Default.aspx

I said, "So do you!" He said, "You know what I mean." "No I don't", I said and I wanted him to specify the issue. "Well", he said, "I won't have a pastor who would do a same sex commitment service, and you did the Reverend's commitment service."

Again Dear Reader, I must explain. A "commitment" service is also called a "Holy Union" service. When a same sex couple desires to make a life long commitment to each other, just as heterosexual couples do when they decide to marry, but the same sex couple finds that it is not legal by most states to "marry", they often plan a "commitment service." These services may include commitment vows, the exchange of rings, prayers and blessings. My friend and teacher, the Reverend, of the *Kerygma* class which Ivan took and loved had asked me to officiate at her commitment service. I said I could not be with her on that day because I had made previous plans to be out of the state. The truth of the matter was, I was too frightened to officiate for fear of what might happen to my clerical standings in the state of Rhode Island. I was a coward.

"Ivan," I said, "I also heard that rumor. I was invited to their commitment service but I was out of town. I wasn't even there." "That is not what I've been told," he bellowed. "You were told wrong, Ivan. It is not that I object to same sex commitment services, but with the witch hunt over the issues of homosexuality and church leadership going on within the American Baptist Churches USA, nationally and locally, I chose not to attend. I know my absence hurt the Reverend's feelings. I think that my decision to not attend the service has jeopardized our friendship because I did not have the moral courage to attend her service. You will have to believe me." "Well, it's not what I heard!

Also, I didn't like the sermon you preached several years ago when you mentioned the need for inclusion of homosexuals in church affairs and your concerns over the open and affirming issues raging in the denomination. I won't have it! Not from the pulpit of a church that I'm attending! We are leaving." There was much more said. But we ended the conversation and concluded our meeting in this manner:

1. He promised, unilaterally, that this conversation would stay between us for the sake of the congregation. He agreed and promised that he would not spread rumors and gossip.
2. There was an upsetting issue going on at that time in the GBC choir, and since his wife was part of the choir, he agreed that this

choir upset/issue would be the reason given for their leave taking and transfer of membership to the other church.

3. We agreed to disagree over the issue of homosexuality in civil and theological terms and also to grant, each to the other, a respect for our personal differences of theological interpretation. We agreed to disagree as to whether homosexuality is an issue of nature or nurture or a combination of both. We agreed to disagree on whether homosexuality is the unforgivable sin or not, or even if it is a sin at all. We agreed to disagree on whether the few verses of homosexual condemnation in the Bible were to be held as the sole moral, theological and civil authority for the exclusion of homosexuals from the church and society and especially from leadership positions within and outside of the church.
4. We agreed that we each held our opinions sincerely and honestly and that we believed we were both following Scripture as directed by the Holy Spirit.

I offered to pray as we parted. We held hands and I prayed. I blessed him with:

> *"The Lord bless you and keep you*
> *The Lord make His face to shine upon you and be gracious to you*
> *The Lord lift up His countenance upon you and give you peace,*
> *this day and every*
> *Day"*

We hugged and kissed and he walked out of my life. Or at least so I thought. Several weeks later the Associate Minister of GBC came to me and told me that Ivan had been making phone calls to various parishioners about my "life style." So much for Ivan's promises and agreements! There were "parking lot" gatherings and conversations after church services and the "issue" was beginning to take on a life of its own. A "whisper campaign" had begun. The Associate Minister said, "You're in trouble here and I'm not sure I can be of any help to you." It was becoming obvious to me that the Adult Sunday school, now under the sole leadership of the Moderator, was also instrumental in stirring the pot against me.

I was faced with a choice. Should I confront this small minority of malcontents and address their concerns in a private meeting where I could address the few, or should I call for a vote of confidence with the entire congregation? I knew from reading the literature and from discussions with other colleagues that once a pastor calls for a congregational vote of confidence, even though the pastor wins the vote, the ministry is most often over within the next several years.

Did I want to drag my family through a nasty and ridiculous "hearing" and a vote? I felt confident I would win the vote because there were only a few malcontents, but my victory would come at a great emotional price to me, to my children, to my companion, to her children, to her mother, to my father and to the countless friends I had at GBC. The emotional costs were too staggering to even contemplate or consider.

And so, at the Executive Board meeting of GBC, in February 2001, the leaders of the church let me know by their lack of enthusiasm for my plans for Easter (that I had just outlined) and by their body language and spoken word that things were not well with the "health" of the church, I offered to resign. And no one, not one person, not one of my closest friends, not a soul at that table on that night said a word. For some reason, at this very critical time in my life, I thought of this situation as . . . the old gospel song goes, they "said not a mumblin word. Not a word, not a word, not a word, not a word."

I knew at that very moment I had lost the church leadership's confidence (at least the officers who were present that awful night) and my unprepared verbal resignation was accepted by those present at the table. The chairs of the Boards of Missions and Christian Education were missing as well as the Associate Minister. I've often wondered had those three persons been at the table if the outcome of the meeting would have been the same. Once my resignation was accepted, I gave the leadership and the congregation three months notice and my last Sunday in the pulpit was the Memorial Day week-end of May, 2001—twelve years almost to the day, of my accepting the congregation's vote to become the Pastor of the Greenville Baptist Church.

I was not the only one who said not a "mumblin word." I became the "sacrificial lamb," and even though I was numbed by the event, and knew that I was being slaughtered on the altar of hypocrisy, even I did not say a word. I had never mentioned the "back room" politics to anyone in the church nor did I speak from the pulpit about my sense of betrayal and lack of confidence from the Executive Board. I knew the congregation was mystified when they heard about my resignation when it was read to them by the Moderator of the church. Still, not one person came to my defense nor did anyone "utter a mumblin word." Perhaps because this congregation had experienced the loss of other beloved pastors who had been forced to resign and they were too timid to fight the "establishment." Perhaps this timid congregation was not willing to try and stop this injustice and they remained the great silent majority or they simply didn't care.

There was not a "mumblin word" from the denomination, nor from the Executive Minister . . . no words of comfort, no words of help, no visits, no phone calls . . . just total silence. I wondered to myself, "is this the Christian attitude that I have adopted as my life's blood?"

There was not a "mumblin word" from most of my colleagues, with the exception of Tom Bichan and the pastor who followed him at Chepachet Union Church. Both of these men came to the Lake House, called "Angels Rest" and offered prayers and comfort. Everyone else was silent. I did receive a phone call from a colleague who said kind words and then added, "I had several people come to me and express their concerns months ago." I said to him that it was a little like having the horse outside the barn to tell me now: "Why didn't you call me then and at the very least to warn me to watch my back?" He had no answer! Not another "mumblin word."

Except for family and the nearest and dearest of friends I was alone, abandoned, wounded and comfortless. For weeks and months, the various and many scenarios of the buildup to this momentous occasion in my life swirled through my mind as I tried to self-analyze what it was that had actually happened. Even I was in a quandary as to the events that had caused this earthquake in my life.

Every year when the Passion of Christ is read, I think to myself, "Jesus was betrayed with a kiss by a trusted and loyal friend, an apostle, and very shortly thereafter, by the other apostles who also deserted Him. He was left all alone, with the exception of a few women who followed him to the cross." And then I say to myself, "If they could do this to Jesus, who am I to be treated any differently?"

They led Him to Pilate's bar
Not a word, not a word, not a word, not a word
They led Him to Pilate's bar
Not a word, not a word, not a word, not a word
They led Him to Pilate's bar
But He never said a mumblin' word
Not a word, not a word, not a word, not a word

They all cried, "Crucify Him" . . .

They nailed Him to the tree . . .

They pierced Him in the side . . .

He hung His head and died . . .

Wasn't that a pity and a shame . . .

PART FOUR

Resurrection and the Berean Baptist Church

"He hung His head and died . . . .
But He never said a mumbling word
Not a word, not a word, not a word, not a word
Wasn't that a pity and a shame."

And so ends the Negro Spiritual. Not a word is sung, nor implied, that Jesus had the Last Word on the morning of the Resurrection. Yet He arose, betrayal and death, pity and shame did not have the final word.

If I left the essay *Friendship and Betrayal* as the last chapter for my memoirs, Dear Reader, it would be a pity and a shame, because then you would never know that I found life after death from the Greenville Baptist Church. Today, as I write with GBC behind me, I know that I have achieved "resurrection." It took many months of deep mourning, soul searching, prayer, tears, pharmaceuticals and living as if I were wandering in the wilderness. I declined any preaching invitations. I moved my church membership to the Oak Lawn Community Baptist Church where my companion and friend, Phyllis, was the pastor, and I joined the sanctuary choir. I sang my way to partial wholeness. The good folk at Oak Lawn ministered to me with their unconditional love and support.

During those months of drifting in the wilderness, Phyllis and I invited ten friends to join us for soup and worship on Saturday evenings. We called ourselves **The Congregation in Harmony**, a play on words. We were in spiritual and emotional harmony, and we gathered at our lakeside home in Harmony, RI. We studied scripture, shared a meal and broke bread together at the Lord's Table—We found Peace! These ten other folk had been members of Greenville Baptist Church and all grieved, as did

I, at the way I was treated. **The Congregation in Harmony** was, as one member wrote to me, "*a chance to gather, to share, to weep and hopefully to give some hope and reparation for you. It certainly will always remain in my heart as a time set apart, so unique in fellowship and learning. So holy.*"

The time in the wilderness began the healing process and laid the groundwork for my first position as an Interim Minister. In January 2001, I had successfully completed sixty hours of Basic Education in the dynamics of interim ministry offered by *Interim Ministry Network.*[26] The course began in 2000. I took the course, with eventual retirement in mind, because I knew that both denominations, with which I was affiliated, required this intensive course of two semesters as a requirement if a pastor wanted to pursue Interim Ministry as a vocation or after retirement. I had taken the course that was being offered in Connecticut and figured that when I was ready to retire from Greenville Baptist I would have the required credentials. Little did I know in January 2001 that I would be resigning the pulpit at Greenville in May of that year!

Sometime in late November or early December of 2001 my friend, the Reverend Tom Bichan, came to call. He and his wife, Maria, had stayed in touch with me and I know they held me in prayer. Tom was serving the Berean Baptist Church in Harrisville, RI as the Interim Minister following his retirement from the Chepachet Union Church. Tom loved the little congregation. He said to me once, "Lynne, every time I drive by that dear little church in Harrisville, I want to get my hands on it and bring it back to its former beauty." And he did! He and Maria spent hours repairing the building, refurbishing the sanctuary, the bathrooms, the halls, the kitchen, and the gathering rooms downstairs. They rallied the congregation to take responsible ownership of their property. The lawns were mowed and the flower gardens planted. After several years of Tom's leadership The Berean Baptist Church was once again a thriving community of faith. The congregation grew in numbers as well as in faith. The congregation began to reach out to their community in several ways. And now Tom was tired. He told me on that visit that his cancer had returned. He wanted to stay with this congregation, and worship with them, but not as their pastor. He asked, "Would you consider becoming the new Interim Minister once I retired again?" This is the second time in my life that a pastor had asked

[26] Interim Ministry Network 5740 Executive Drive, Suite 220 Baltimore, MD 21228

me to help lead a congregation while the pastor and his family remained in the congregation. You will recall-The Pendleton Hill Church and now Berean Baptist.

I was hesitant. When I was asked by Dick Mitchell to come to Pendleton Hill I was an enthusiastic student in training. When asked by Tom Bichan, 20 years later, I was not very enthusiastic about stepping back in the pulpit and into a leadership position after the crucifixion of Greenville. I said I would have to pray about the matter.

Tom had the Moderator, Royal, of the Berean Church, take me to lunch. I went. He talked—I listened. I said, "Royal, have you heard all the rumors about me from the Greenville Baptist Church?' He replied, "I have." "And you still want me to come to Berean?" I said rather mystified. "Yes," he said. "I'll never forget the Baptism Class that you designed and taught. My son was in your class: i.e. the joint baptismal class with Chepachet Union and Greenville. My wife and I had to come to that first meeting with the candidates. I appreciated you then, and Pastor Tom speaks very highly of you. That is good enough for me." "And is it good enough for the Berean congregation?" I asked. His reply was very simple, "Yes!"

I began my "second career" in ministry as an intentional interim minister at the Berean Baptist Church on January 2, 2002. I was there for twelve months. During that year my spirit was renewed, and my faith in the goodness of God's people was revived and restored. I don't believe I ever lost my devotion to Christ, but I did lose my devotion to His church. The little congregation of the Berean Baptist Church in Harrisville, RI was the instrument God used to help bring me back to help lead Christ's church.

It was a wonderful year. I made many friends. When the congregation "Called" their new pastor, who happened to be my son-in-law, I knew I was ready to move on and take another interim position. Little did I know that I would have to wait eleven months before the next call! Talk about trying to learn how to live in ambiguity: no job and no money and absolutely no help from the denomination I had faithfully served for 21 years.

I returned to the sanctuary choir at Oak Lawn and sang while I waited for the next "Interim Call." It came in November, 2003 from the Second Congregational Church of Attleboro, United Church of Christ, MA. It was worth the wait

Second Congregational Church, United Church of Christ, of Attleboro

Where do I begin to tell you, Dear Reader, the love, peace and joy that I received while I served as Interim Pastor of the Second Congregational Church? My arrival at Second was another miracle in my life.

I am told that "Second," as it is affectionately called, was without an Interim Pastor for over 6 months. Apparently, the search committee had interviewed some candidates, but either the candidate took another position or the candidate was not compatible with the Search Committee. There were great frustrations within the Search Committee. During this 6 month hiatus, the Director of Christian Education and Minister of Family Life, the Reverend Ruth Shaver, was acting as interim pastor along with handling her own responsibilities. The Area Minister had no further names to submit to the committee, and, as I understand it, he called the UCC Executive Minister of Rhode Island and asked if there was anyone from Rhode Island he might recommend to the search committee of Second Congregational. My name was recommended and, as grace would have it, I was asked to interview for the position of Interim Pastor.

The interview went well and I was asked to preach to a select group of parishioners on a Wednesday evening. I agreed to come and lead the parishioners in a worship service, but I said I would not come just to "preach." The search committee was a little taken aback with my comment, but they agreed. I went and led worship with prayers, hymns and a sermon based on the weekly lectionary text. The next day I received the "Call" to become the Interim Pastor and I held that position for almost four years.

There was much unhappiness and dissension within the congregation when I began my work in November, 2004. There were divisions within the congregation, camps if you will, which prevented the congregation from knowing good health and wholeness. The church was like the early church in Corinth where there were factions and parties and different loyalties. At Second, there were some parishioners who loved and mourned the former pastor's leaving while other parishioners had left the church in hopes that the former pastor would leave. There were loyalties toward various leaders within the congregation, and there were former teachers/ pastors whose influence was always surfacing and interfering with the life of the congregation. There was some indifference and even sullenness among the parishioners within the pews on the Sunday I first appeared to lead in worship. There they sat! Hands folded; faces grim. Some looked as if they were sitting on a broom stick. The "Frozen Chosen" had come to check me out!

I had been hired to work with all the boards and committees during the month of November and prepare the themes and the agenda for Advent, but my first Sunday in the pulpit was not until the first Sunday of December, 2004. I came to the pulpit holding a typical kitchen broom made of straw. I told the congregation that my broom was a symbol of my transitory tenure and that I would sweep in, sweep out and clean house in between and that when I left I would take my broom with me.

I told the congregation that as an "Intentional Interim Minister," a term that reflects my special training and duties, I would help guide them through a self-examination process and I would help the congregation find wholeness and health if they were willing. I told them I would work with the search committee up to the point that their church profile was ready to present. I also told the congregation that I would help them be prepared to welcome the new pastor when that time came. Little did I know that all that sweeping, guiding, healing, and helping to prepare would take us all of four years to complete the interim tasks.

When pastors leave the role of pastor of a particular church under the best of circumstances, congregations need to grieve, and also to do some self-examination. When I am hired to be an Intentional Interim Minister I see myself as being a non anxious presence, a calming influence in a sea of anxiety and mixed emotions within the congregation.

There is nothing more upsetting to a congregation than to lose a pastor, no matter the circumstances. The congregation reels when it happens and all kinds of emotions are present within the congregation. In some cases, there will be happiness that the pastor finally left, and in other cases, there will be sadness and perhaps bitterness that the pastor felt forced to leave. There will always be anxiety among some parishioners who will wonder what will become of the congregation and finally this unspoken concern, "will anyone ever love us again?" The congregation will also experience grief that the divisions within the church have split friendships and, in some cases, families. There is always the hope that the new pastor will meet the needs of the youth and the elderly and all those in between. On and on emotions build. The natural tendency for any congregation whose pastor has retired, or left for another position, or died in office or even was fired, is to jump right in and fill the vacuum by hiring a new pastor. Experience has proven that that would not be good for the congregation.

What the congregation needs to do instead is to assess and analyze where it has been, where it is and where it wants to be. By making that assessment and analysis, the congregational members can determine what type of leadership they will need for the future. One of the advantages of being an interim minister is that my job does not depend on the members liking my critique and that allows me to be more forthright and say the things that a permanent pastor might be reluctant to say. In the congregations where I have served as interim pastor I have found the freedom to be me; to laugh, to love and to live the gospel to the best of my ability knowing that I will be leaving and taking my broom with me. All of my interim positions have been liberating, satisfying and fun. In turn, I hope I was able to teach these congregations that humor is great, the gospel is good and their congregation was ready to move on.

Over time the good folk at Second Congregational began to trust me and also to trust in my leadership skills. There had been very little trust for some previous resident pastors over the years. We don't need to go into those reasons, but the remarkable thing is that during our time together trust was established and the congregation was beginning to heal and reach out beyond itself.

This particular congregation worshiped in a beautiful downtown red brick edifice with magnificent stained glass windows and the finest architectural embellishments that old money could buy. The building was a monument to the late industrial barons of Attleboro. It was perceived by those outside of the congregation as "The Place" where the "elite" went to worship. Those golden days of the early twentieth century were gone and the congregation that was worshipping in this magnificent building was almost a cross section of the Attleboro area. Perceptions are hard to change. When I first came to Attleboro and began to visit parishioners and have ecumenical dialogs with other pastors in the area, plus make acquaintances with the local business people, I learned that many of these folk still saw the Second Congregational Church as "The Church of the affluent." There was a grain of truth to that perception: the building was impressive . . . is impressive. The music was exceptional . . . is exceptional. The congregation always has paid handsomely for their music program with paid section leaders in their choir and the music at Second Congregational was extraordinary. Even during troubling times of the past, it was the Director of Music and the musicians who offered stability and continuity to the congregation.

But when I arrived, the congregation, as a unified worshipping group, was ill. It was divided and too disturbed to be "The Church" where one wanted to attend, with or without money. There was much work to be done. After we developed a level of trust between pastor and people the tide began to turn . . . for the better. Members who had left the congregation began to return, new members joined, young families began to attend and the Sunday school began to truly flourish under the guidance of Rev. Ruth. I tried to inspire the congregation and her leaders to go beyond what they thought they were capable of and go beyond their comfort zones which included their first short term mission trip to Appalachia. It was a nudge out the door of what was familiar and known! I felt it was my task and pleasure to help the members of the congregation to rediscover the fundamental elements of their faith and how they were to practice them in their daily lives. I had to remind the congregation of the uniqueness and inclusiveness of their Congregational heritage. But the most important thing I try to do whenever I enter an interim position, aside from my assessments, gaining trust, and attend to the basic pastoral tasks, is to simply love the members of the congregation. When I first came to the church, the people at Second were divided, contentious with each other, dispirited and depressed. By the time the New Pastor was "called" the congregation knew they were loved by God and by me. Healing and wholeness came by the grace of God, my hard work as interim pastor and the cooperation of the people, and the congregation's willingness to heal and learn new ways of living together.

By the time it was necessary for me to leave, it was I who had to grieve. I had come to love this congregation in ways I had never loved before and I saw the resurrection of a dying church come to life before my very eyes.

My next interim call was to a small Baptist church on Block Island, Rhode Island with 12 miles of the Atlantic Ocean separating me from land, my home and the friends at Second. Even as I write this memoir I knew, on my first trip to the Island, that I was not sailing to Block Island in great anticipation and hope. I knew that I was running away from Second. I left my heart at Second. My separation from Second was almost like two lovers being forced to separate by parental standards: that is, the United Church of Christ is very firm in its By-laws that Interim Pastors may not become the permanent pastor, regardless of the length of their service or the bond between pastor and people.

At my last Sunday in the pulpit, with much laughter and tears, the moderator came to the lectern and read the following:

> *"Finally, we need to express to you in the most sincere way we know how that you will always be held in great esteem by us, and that you will be remembered as one of the great Pastors who has served this church. We believe that there can be no distinction here between "Interim" and "Permanent". With this in mind, it is our pleasure to inform you that Second Congregational Church, UCC, of Attleboro, Massachusetts has bestowed upon you the permanent designation of 'Pastor Emerita'."*

Block Island, Rhode Island - My Experience

Block Island, Rhode Island is almost 12 miles out to sea and directly south of the Rhode Island shoreline. There are times when no one can get to or off of this "pork chop" shaped piece of land due to severe weather. No planes can land and the Interstate Navigation's Block Island Ferry will not run when weather conditions are too bad. One learns to cope when isolated on an island! On Ground Hog Day, the island locals conduct their own census. On February 2, 2009 there were 1,021 people living, working, going to school, or retired on the island. This is true almost every winter, i.e. the tourists move off the Island, and the locals get it back for themselves. Block Island is also known as the "Bermuda of the North." Block Island is listed by *The Nature Conservancy* as one of "The Last Great Places" on earth, one of only twelve such designations in the western Hemisphere. I had the privilege to serve 14 months as Interim Pastor of the First Baptist Church of Block Island, commonly known as The Harbor Church.

I went to my first interview for the position of Interim Pastor kicking and screaming. The Executive Minister of the American Baptist Churches of Rhode Island had asked me to interview for the position. She knew I was leaving Second Congregational Church, Attleboro, and she wanted me at Harbor Church. I said I wasn't too interested in leaving home and staying on the island. I would miss my family and the comfort of my bed! It would be an impossible daily commute by plane or ferry. And I was still emotionally tied to Second Congregational. As I wrote previously, I was not running toward Block Island, I was running away from Second!

I agreed to have an interview, knowing in the back of my mind that I would say "NO" and hopefully be offered another Interim position on Cape Cod where I had interviewed several days prior to my trip to BI. I went. I wasn't excited, but I went as a favor to the Executive Minister. I was familiar with the church and the apartment which the church provided because I had acted as supply preacher when their pastor had taken her month vacation in 2002 and 2003. I knew many of the parishioners. My concern was living alone on BI and away from my family and friends for an extended period of time.

When the time came for me to meet with the deacons of the church, I recognized several of the deacons from my previous island stays. The Chair of the Deacons opened with prayer and set the agenda for the interview. Two of the young men who were deacons were new to me. I was asked a variety of questions, and I tried to answer the best I could. I gave this interview my all! I was pleasant, engaging, and humorous at times, and I showed that I had experience as a trained Interim Pastor.

One of the younger deacons asked me to give my "testimony" and to tell the board when I was "saved." I didn't know that I had been "lost" but I spoke of my spiritual formation and journey. I don't talk about "being saved" but I do talk about having a "personal relationship" with the Lord. The deacon said that my answer wasn't sufficient and would I please comment on my "salvation" story. I reiterated my first response and indicated I was unsure of what he wanted. I believed that I was "saved" but that I couldn't state a day or time of my "conversion."

The tone of the interview was deteriorating rapidly. Then he said, "By what authority do you think you are called to preach?" He had been pushing my buttons, so to speak, most of the evening. I answered I was ordained to preach the gospel and that I was one of the best preachers he was going to hear. Not very modest, I know, but I was angry. A deacon who had been active when I had served as substitute preacher in 2002 and 2003 spoke up and said, "She is right! She is an outstanding preacher! I know! I've heard her." Bless her heart. This older deacon was not one to be so outspoken. To make a long story short, I was excused, and the board voted to ask me to be the Interim Pastor and the two young male deacons voted no. The one that gave me the hardest time, i.e. my antagonist, said, "I'm not going to have some middle aged woman tell me what to do!"

Meanwhile, as I was waiting to hear about the Board of Deacon's vote, I said to my friend Phyllis, "I'm not coming here! Who needs this aggravation?"

I was told of the Board's positive vote, and I politely said that I needed to think about it. Then I was rushed off to dinner and then to another meeting, but this time with the Search Committee which had been formed even before the settled Pastor had taken leave and before the Executive Minister could help them with the selection process. I knew some of the members on this committee, and we made small talk before the chair called the meeting to order. What happened then was the presentation of a litany of troubles this committee perceived in regards to the poor health of the church, the finances of the church, the effect of isolation from island living, and the need for the church to draw back members who had left. This group of people felt the pews had been emptied out and they had very little hope or ideas on how to rejuvenate the congregation. It was a very sad meeting! There was little joy in the group. There was no vision in the group aside from the "good old days with Tony," a former Pastor. I had already made up my mind that I didn't want to put up with the narrow views of some of the deacons and that I was no longer interested in fighting the "woman pastor" issues again, nor battle between the conservative and liberal Christians in regards to Biblical authority, nor struggle with trying to put "Humpty Dumpty back together again." And then . . . without warning I heard my lips say to the Search Committee, "Don't do anything until I get here!" And then I knew I was going to Block Island.

I originally went to Block Island kicking and screaming, and I ended up having one of the most interesting times of my life. I discovered how much I loved and enjoyed island life. I developed friendships with a group of women NOT connected with the church and these friendships continue to feed my soul. I met extraordinary people from all walks of life. I fell in love with the Block Island community. And, I loved the natural and aesthetic beauty of the island itself. Those 14 months were some of the happiest months of my lifelong ministry and were some of the most fruitful. I was saddened by the fact that the two younger deacons decided to worship elsewhere while I was the Interim. There are always transitions during the interim period. It was my task to be steadfast in my faith and to be a non-anxious, calming, if you will, presence as parishioners and pastor worked through those transitional issues. It was one of my tasks to help the congregation prepare itself to welcome a new permanent pastor. In 14 short months the congregation was ready to welcome Rev. Steve.

Block Island surreptitiously and subtly snags you . . . you fall under its spell and you never want to leave . . . and even after you do leave, you are drawn back like so much flotsam and jetsam washed up on the shore. Block Island **is** one of the last great places on the earth!

A Romp Around Rebecca

The resident Block Island Episcopalians had gathered for their monthly potluck supper. For this particular gathering, we were meeting at the home of Pam and Jim. Although I was not a member of the congregation of St. Ann's-By-The-Sea, I was always invited to the monthly potluck suppers, and for the most part, I went. These monthly gatherings were wonderful social affairs. Father Dan and his wife Meg had become my good friends during my 14 months as the resident interim pastor on Block Island. Episcopalians don't have any of the "hang-ups" about alcohol that the Baptists have. Oh, many Baptists enjoy an alcoholic beverage and some even go to the bars or order a glass of wine when they are publicly out for dinner, but at a church function, or any function held in or on church property, no alcohol would ever be served!

I have a Methodist pastor friend and he told me that his ordination vows include abstinence from alcohol, but his wife will remind him that, "I didn't take those vows." She will order a glass of wine at a restaurant, but she will ask to have the wine served in a cup or colored glass . . . this to "protect" her husband's reputation. All this is to say, that at the monthly potlucks sponsored by St. Ann's-by-the-Sea, the alcohol flows freely, and I would have a glass or two of wine.

As I said, Jim and Pam were hosting the December potluck dinner. We were to gather earlier than usual because we were to go caroling to the shut-ins on the island. We loaded up the cars and went down Corn Neck Road stopping to sing at a home near the Labyrinth. Our little caravan stopped at several more places to sing to shut-ins, and then we backtracked to the center of town. We parked in the town parking area opposite the statue of Rebecca at the bottom of the hill where the Harbor Baptist Church is located. Jim opened the back of his vehicle and Bill opened the back of his van and refreshments were served. We had a choice of hot chocolate, mulled cider or mulled wine. With a hot drink in hand, someone suggested we gather around the stature of Rebecca and sing a carol or two. Once the mulled wine took its warming effects, the singing became louder and we began to dance and might I add, romp, around Rebecca, singing, "We wish you a Merry Christmas." Fortunately for us there was no reporter from the *Block Island Times* to record that the Reverend Father Dan Barker, the Reverend Dr. Lynne Holden and a heavenly host of their parishioners were last seen romping around the statue of Rebecca with drinks in hand. I think the better choice of carol to be sung, had we known the words, would have been from "Good King Wenceslas."

Bring me flesh, and bring me wine.
Bring me pine logs hither . . . .

Sire, the night is darker now,
And the wind blows stronger.
Fails my heart, I know not how.
I can go no longer . . . .

It was dark and the wind did blow and we had a wonderful time singing, dancing and drinking to Rebecca, "until we could go no longer." Now why such glee? Because the statue of Rebecca which stands at the foot of the Baptist Church at the intersection of Water, High and Spring Streets was originally erected in 1896 by the Women's Christian Temperance Union (WCTU). This statue was dedicated to the abstinence of alcohol. The WCTU women believed that there was simply too much drinking of "spirits" on the island in 1896. I suppose they researched various statue catalogs and liked this model of a stately, properly draped woman, carrying a jug. If you study this stark white statue you can see the wreath of grapes that encircle her head. The statue was once, indeed, a working water fountain. There were troughs for dogs and horses and a fountain for the good folk of the island offering cold running water. These troughs today are planted with seasonal flowers. The women of the WCTU assumed this statue represented the Biblical Rebekah-at-the Well. As the story is told, according to Block Island legend and history, this much loved statue was recast and reinstalled to celebrate her 100th anniversary. The conservationists who did the work in 1996 concluded that the woman portrayed in the statue was not Rebekah—at-the Well, but rather Hebe, cupbearer to the gods.

The statue of Rebecca, erected and dedicated to the abstinence of alcohol, turns out to be the "cup bearer to the gods," a cup bearer of wine, not water: a travesty to the memory of the Block Island WCTU. On Block Island the statue of Rebecca regally stands, grapes woven around her head, she holding her jug with both hands, tipping down, pouring her libation out over the town. And on a special night in December of 2008, two parsons and two carloads of parishioners raised their cups to her, laughed and sang and had a good romp at the expense of the Women's Christian Temperance Union at the foot of the hill of the Baptist Church where I was serving as Interim Pastor.

A Grand Block Island Experience

It was a night unlike any I had ever experienced before, and I dare say will never experience again. I was the guest of Father Dan and his wife, Meg, and I was with them to attend a fund raiser sponsored by St. Ann's by-the-Sea Episcopal Church. Father Dan was the Interim Pastor at St. Ann's by the Sea. The fund raiser was billed as "Classics by Candlelight." Dan and Meg picked me up in their new Lincoln Town Car, and we drove to the west side of Block Island. Dan had to navigate this beautiful car over narrow dirt roads with pot holes and wash outs deep enough to land us in China. At one point I was fearful that the shrubs along the drive would scrape and scar the car. The car dragged bottom over a long dirt driveway where the mower had obviously missed the center of the two ruts known as a "private drive". I spotted a large house, a mansion in my estimation, off in the distance, facing the Atlantic Ocean and I said to Meg, "Look at that place over there!" She replied that that was where we were going. We were going to that gorgeous waterfront home for an evening of chamber music.

When we drove up to the front door, my friend, Jim, met us, opened the car door for Father Dan, and another man from the Episcopal congregation opened the doors for Meg and me. Jim parked the beautiful Lincoln down the hill on manicured lawns. I saw Hank pick off four or five imperfect hydrangea leaves in the front garden and he was holding these leaves as we greeted each other. We were graciously received at the door by Mike H. with kisses for Meg and me and a warm welcome for Father Dan. I asked Mike where his wife Elisa was. "In the kitchen," he replied. I didn't give that a second thought since Elisa spends the bulk of her time shopping, organizing and delivering food through the Helping Hands Ministries that Harbor Church and St. Ann's have been running for several years. I figured that Elisa must be helping Anna Marie, the mistress of the house.

As Dan and Meg were visiting with others, I spotted Jim's wife, Pam, down the hall, and I went to greet her. She was wearing a black dress and white apron with cut-out lace trimming the bottom and top of the apron. She looked lovely and introduced herself to me as the "French maid." I spotted Sue in black slacks and white top and then Hank's wife, Toni, in a simple white dress, and they seemed to be busy in and out of the kitchen. Light bulbs started going off in my head. In order for St. Ann's to pull this fund raiser off, many of the parishioners had to work "behind the scenes" as valets, gardeners, servers, and kitchen crew. I felt as if I should have been in the kitchen with them. I felt out of my league.

Before the evening of music began, I went out to the patio admiring the beautiful sunset over the ocean, the incredible lawns and I took a photo of the flower arrangement surrounded by champagne glasses. Montauk, on the eastern tip of Long Island, NY, could be seen on the far horizon. What an incredible sight: land, sea, sunset, and the incredible detail in arrangement of flowers and glasses. I felt I had just stepped into Fitzgerald's *The Great Gatsby.* What a fabulous piece of real estate. And there is no way I could begin to describe the home. The foyer was three stories tall!

The evening began. The living room was filled with chairs borrowed from Harbor Church. All of the exquisite furniture that I had seen in this same room back in January, when I was there for a potluck supper, had been removed. The focal point of the room was the grandest Grand Piano I have ever seen. The solid legs of the piano are carved to represent intricate columns of 3 balls balanced upon each other. Even before one can hear a sound, the magnificence of the instrument is awe inspiring. This particular instrument is the grandest piano I've ever seen in any church or European cathedral or at the music department of Yale. During the intermission I spoke to Anna Marie about the magnificent piano and she said, "I don't deserve it. I didn't start playing until I was 47 years old. It means so much to me to hear it played by Paul," (the artist for the evening.) Paul surely made the piano come alive.

The Classics by Candlelight was an evening of piano, violin and clarinet music performed by experts. I was prepared not to like the first Sonata for Violin and Piano written by a Czech composer after the violinist explained the minutia of the piece. She said she hoped it wasn't "too much past our comfort zone." Oh dear! But as the various pieces progressed I was very captivated by the music. And all the while they played, I thought, "This is a fabulous way to spend a summer evening. This is right out of the movies or a book." I pictured New Yorkers or Newport socialites gathered in someone's grand penthouse or salon being entertained by musicians. And here I sat surrounded by the beauty of the grounds, the grandness of the home and the quality of music being offered. I felt I was in a fairy tale . . . would I turn into a pumpkin at midnight? I felt as though, at any minute, the "Great Gatsby" might walk into the room!

During intermission we had champagne and hors d'oevres on the patio, served by my friends from St. Ann's, Toni, Sue, and Pam. Elisa was, indeed, in the kitchen, keeping the trays of hors d'oevres hot and coming. I am not partial to champagne. The only time I have champagne is at a wedding when we all toast the bride and groom, and then I never touch my glass again. But this champagne was delicious, fabulous, extraordinary! When I told Father Dan how much I liked it he said, "It's Brut." Brut—snoot—it didn't matter. It was far better than any wedding champagne I had ever tasted!

The second half of the program featured the clarinet. As an amateur clarinetist myself, I was particularly interested in the Clarinetist's handling of the instrument. He was outstanding. I began playing the clarinet when I was in the fourth grade, and I continued through college. The experience of learning how to read music and the discipline of practice were important lessons for me. I gave my clarinet away when I was teaching at Pine Point to a young woman who was just beginning her musical journey. I hope she enjoyed it as much as I did. But back to the evening of Classics by Candlelight. The second half of the evening was as enjoyable as the first half maybe even more so after two glasses of champagne. We finished the evening with outlandishly decadent desserts.

Back to my apartment on Block Island, awash in visions of a simple gal having spent an evening in such luxury and beauty, I knew this would be one of my favorite memories of my year on Block Island, what I call a true Block Island experience.

It's Tuesday

Tuesday was my second favorite day of the week on Block Island. As a preacher, I have to say that Sunday was my favorite day, which is true, because that was the day when I saw the entire community of faith. While I was on Block Island, especially Tuesdays during the summer months, I began setting my alarm for 6:30 a.m. every Tuesday so that I could get to the Bird Banding lessons at the Conservation Pavilion. There Kim taught me how to hold a bird. Imagine! It took 67 years for me to be brave enough to let a bird get close to me, let alone have a bird sit in my hand. I was very proud of myself.

During the winter and off-season months, I went to the Senior Center for the Lunch Bunch where we had the most delicious meals for the princely sum of $4.00. That hardly covers a hot dog anywhere on the island in the summertime, and there is no place to even buy a hot dog in the winter. Following lunch on Tuesdays, I was then off to play Bridge, and I ended the day with singing in the Ecumenical Choir. Tuesday was my favorite day!

At 10 a.m. on Tuesdays I would leave my upstairs apartment in the Harbor Church and go downstairs to the Ladies' Parlor next to the sanctuary to join with the Memoirs Group. I loved meeting with Edie, Eleanor, Sandy, Martha and Ellen. A typical Tuesday Memoirs gathering might start something like this:

> "Sorry I'm late," says Edie, breathlessly. "I had to take a phone call just as I was leaving the office. You can't imagine the problem this time." "Tell, Tell," we all cry out together. The problems that Edie would relate to us about summer renters on the island kept us in stitches. "Today, a man called and said

> he couldn't stay in his rental because there were spiders in the house and his little girls were afraid of spiders." Once Edie told us about a man who called and said the back door squeaked and would she come over with WD40 and fix it. "No," was her reply. Another time someone called because the house didn't have a blender. So Edie took over her very own blender. We all liked to hear her tales about the renters: most of them were spoiled and expecting Edie to be at their beck and call.

We love hearing Edie's Block Island stories, such as where she was and what she was doing during the 1938 hurricane. I remember how she said her mother saw their outhouse fly off and not too soon later, another outhouse flew back into their yard. Lose some-win some. Between Edie's and Eleanor's stories we were given a glimpse of Block Island life before this tiny piece of land became a destination place for the wealthy, the retired and a summer haven for those who love the sand and sea. Edie and Eleanor were school friends, and they continue to be friends after all these years. They have shared common histories. They have been there for each other during joyous times and during very sad times. They have been together on the island raising their children, maintaining their homes, each living on ancestral real estate. On Block Island, in order to be considered a "native" one must have been born on the Island. They were "natives"!

Some of my favorite sayings I've heard from Eleanor and Edie are these:

> "Women can do anything and sometimes they have to."
> When you winterize the house for the winter, it was said by someone, "The house won't eat or drink all winter."

"Gap and shallow" is a spoon dish, i.e. soup or stew.

"Cheeks and sounds" or "cheeks and tongue" is a chowder type of meal made from a codfish head.

Eleanor's husband was a fisherman, but apparently he wasn't too fond of cheeks and sounds.

We always took turns reading to each other the page or two of reflections which we had written to be read for that day. We tried to not "go against the sun" when it was our turn to read. That was a rule Edie's father instilled in her. I'll never forget the time Eleanor was reading and she told us how, as a young girl, no one in her family would explain the "F" word to her. She had seen it somewhere and had asked her mother and sisters what it meant. Only after her persistence did her older sister tell her the following: the "F" word means "found under carnal knowledge." Poor little Eleanor had her answer but it didn't mean a thing to her. We all laughed.

One Tuesday Martha told us that she and her husband Bill had had a special time together and opened a bottle of champagne, "too good for company." I liked that idea. The champagne was so good, why not enjoy it with the most special person in the world. Martha shared with us her life story in a methodical and chronological order. Sometimes Martha thought her stories were too boring and we would not be interested. But we were. Because we were interested in her, her stories were important to us. That is the lovely thing about a Memoirs Group. We developed a trust level and an intimacy among ourselves that made sharing easy, and we were willing to share our stories. Martha holds the honor of being the first of our Memoirs Group of Block Island to have her writings published. The title of her work is "The Time of My Life." We are so very proud of Martha's accomplishments!

Everyone has a story. When you write a memoir, you are the star of the story. And I think one of the beauties of being part of a memoirs group is just that, that is, you are able to share your life and experiences with friends who are doing likewise. One might feel that her story is boring next to Martha's story, someone who has worked with famous scientists and academics, one who has traveled extensively and who is a meticulous grammarian. But that feeling of believing that our stories might be boring would be a falsehood, because as Martha said, "We never apologize, never explain." There is no need to apologize or explain when each person's story is precious and interesting.

In a small group of women who have lived on this island, some of them all their lives, and I for only 14 months, we marveled when our story lines intersected, whether we were talking about a place where we may have lived or worked, or when our experiences had been similar. For instance: Ellen lived in the Morristown Area of N.J. and I worked for 5 summers at the Girl Scout Camp in Sparta, NJ. The camp was operated by the Morristown Area Girl Scout Council, the same council in which Ellen served as a troup leader. Ellen also lived in Ridgefield, CT and I lived in Ridgefield, CT on Lake Mamanasco. Different times, different stories, but our lives intersected in the telling of these stories.

Sandy grew up in Dalton, Ma, and Edie worked in Dalton, MA for a year after her husband died. Sandy and Edie would talk about the mill in Dalton, the town hall . . . an example of the saying: "there is only 6 degrees of separation from everyone." Eleanor's original roots were from Attleboro, MA, and I had just served 4 years as Interim at Second Congregational Church in Attleboro.

We have all laughed and reminisced over favorite Radio and TV shows. I was the youngest member of this particular Memoirs Group, but we shared so many common memories about growing up, school days, parental standards, marriage and child rearing. We had wonderful discussions and readings in regards to the civil rights movement and the period of the Vietnam War.

Sandy wrote, "It's difficult to write about the person I was back in 1952-56 and keep who I am now out of the story." That statement resonated with us all. Several of us had to write down her words. As we shared, intimately, aspects of our individual lives, we came to see most clearly how our place of birth and upbringing, our passions and educational opportunities, or lack of opportunities, our loves and losses, our joys and our sorrows molded us into the women we are today.

When Ellen graduated from Wellesley, she headed for Wall Street as one of the first females in the financial world. She didn't hit a glass ceiling; she helped to create an entirely new room for women. Martha and I hit academic ceilings and we resonated with each other's story of trying to break into a world that had previously been male dominated. Martha worked in the academic and research world, and she faced discrimination as a woman who was seeking to become a full professor. I struggled in the male dominated ministerial world when I was seeking a position, first as a student and then 20 years later as one seeking ordination and placement in the ecclesiastical world. Edie struggled with being a woman and trying to raise her boys as a widow in a world that did not and would not recognize her as "head of household." Eleanor took a more conventional route for employment, that of nurse. And Sandy, married and raising children, hasn't begun to tell her story of seeking employment or electing to be a "stay-at home-mom." Her story is to be continued. That was the fun thing about memoirs, a topic was begun and we all came the following week wondering if there would be a conclusion or closure to that story. Sometimes there was, sometimes we still wait.

We were very attentive when the story was a love story. We trusted each other enough to tell of our first loves, first heart beaks, mature loves, disappointments, betrayals and other losses. Those in our group covered the range of "marital status" asked on all doctors' forms: single, widowed, divorced, and married. Speaking of those forms, when the form asks for sex, I answer yes.

I miss this memoirs group very much. These women were a life line for me while I was away from home, often very lonely and sometimes just plain bored. Yet I would know that at 10 a.m. Tuesday morning I would be with them, listening to the different stories, sometimes laughing, sometimes crying, always attentive.

Sandy was probably our most gifted writer and poet; she majored in writing in college. When Eleanor asked about joining the group, she said she wasn't very good at writing, but she would like to try and I found her writing vibrant and enthralling. Edie worried that since she never really studied writing, nor had she been around the world that she had little to write about. Yet, there was no one who could capture our imagination like Edie with her Block Island stories. Ellen's writing was reflective of Ellen's life, one of many facets, abounding in energy, stories with many plot lines and as the saying goes, many irons in the fire. If I have the energy, drive and passion for life that Ellen has, when I am in my 80s, I will consider myself most fortunate. Martha's stories were rich and diverse. I will never read about or see another monkey without thinking of Martha and her research using monkeys.

These women meant the world to me. They still do! I try to get to Block Island on Tuesdays, when the ferry schedule allows, to share in this Memoirs Group. I am grateful for their inclusion of me, not only now, but also when I first came to Block Island. I am grateful that they laughed at my jokes and encouraged me to continue to be brave and write when writing, for me, was emotionally or spiritually difficult. These women were the first to hear about the hurt that I had experienced at Greenville, a hurt that was so deep and a period of my life I felt I was incapable of writing about. Without their encouragement and acceptance I would not have found the courage and fortitude to share this—no, MY story!

So I thank them, each one of them: Edie, Eleanor, Ellen, Martha and Sandy. You have my Blessings. Keep writing!

Getting Ready for the Inauguration of the 44th President of the United States

I was serving as Interim Pastor at the Harbor Church on Block Island in January, 2009 when then Senator Barack Obama was inaugurated as the 44th President of the United States. As I am sure you know, the presidential inauguration takes place on the official day that the elected President of the United States takes the official oath, and is sworn into office. The inauguration honors the incoming president with formal ceremonies, including: a Presidential Swearing-in Ceremony, an Inaugural Address by the new President, and an Inaugural Parade in Washington DC. On January 20, 2009, this very special day, I watched those formal ceremonies all alone in my apartment at the Harbor Church, surrounded by ghosts and memories of the past: ghosts and memories that helped shape this country and especially this momentous occasion for me and for all the citizens of this wonderful nation. I was so happy I cried!!

I was a young woman during the days of the civil rights movement, and I was soon to be married. Martin Luther King, Jr. had stirred up a great deal of controversy on my college campus, as well as in my home. He was seen as a troublemaker by some and a prophet by others. I honestly didn't know what I thought at that time. My personal life was safe and comfortable. The time frame was in the early 60's.

When I was on the debate team at West Virginia Wesleyan we went to Wake Forest College in North Carolina for a match. Wake Forest is a college for Blacks with an enrollment which excluded Caucasians, or I should say, non-blacks. Actually back in 1962 the term "black" was not used by me or the media. We used the term Negro! Mother insisted we say, "Negro" and not "colored" and we were never allowed to say that dehumanizing term, "nigger." We never heard the term African American, back then, either.

Since Wake Forest was a college of predominately black students we certainly didn't see any signs that read: "Negroes only" or more commonly, "Colored only." But we did see such signs when we made rest stops in the South . . . i.e. signs for segregated bathrooms and segregated drinking fountains, bus seats, etc. I had never noticed, at the time, that restaurants in the south were only for whites. I think I didn't see those things because I wasn't looking for them; having lived my entire life up to that time in the northeast, I was totally unaware that segregation was a problem.

I was with a debate team traveling to various colleges throughout the Northeast and the South, and my focus was to win! So I didn't know that blacks couldn't eat at lunch counters or in restaurants; sit wherever they chose on the bus; or even be admitted to northern colleges that did not have a "quota" system. "Separate but equal" was not part of my vocabulary and during my growing up years I would not have known what that meant.

I had no idea that it was illegal in some States for a white person to marry a black person, nor had I ever heard the word "miscegenation." My neighborhood grammar school had white and black children enrolled. The church that I attended was all white. There were whites and blacks at college in West Virginia. Blacks were on all the teams, in the choirs, in the band, but there were none in the fraternities or sororities. I didn't pay any attention. I wasn't in a sorority either.

Then came the national news broadcasts on TV during the mid 60s. We did not have a color TV, so the videos were in black and white. The news was dominated by the conflict between blacks and whites of that period, and especially about civil unrest. We watched, in horror, as whites held fire hoses on black men, women and children, the force of the water throwing them onto the streets or backing them into buildings. We witnessed white police officers allowing their patrol dogs to rip the clothes and skins of little black children going to "white" schools, as mandated by the US Supreme Court. We saw TV videos on the National news, of blacks staging sit-ins at a lunch counter and marching and singing "We Shall Over Come Someday." We watched as a white governor, holding a baseball bat, stood in the doorway of an all white university, barring the admission of black students.

Emotions were running extremely high everywhere, on the border of hysteria. I have vivid memories of those times. I was not marching in Washington. I was not working for the civil rights movement. I was teaching school at Pine Point, in peaceful Connecticut and trying to help my husband through his Ph.D. program at Brown University in Providence, RI. We were comfortable and secure in our own little world.

But I remember when Martin Luther King, Jr. was assassinated in April, 1968. I remember seeing him deliver his "I Have A Dream Speech" on television and being very moved by it. I remember how stunned I was when the news came through a television broadcast that Dr. King had been killed, and then I remember saying to my husband, "We are going to have hell to pay for this." Then, in June, Robert (Bobbie) Kennedy was assassinated. Two hopefuls for the civil rights movement, a black man and a white man had been killed.

We were with friends, having dinner, when the 1968 National Democratic Convention was being televised. Hubert Humphrey and Ed Muskie were the Democratic nominees that year. The convention was being held in Chicago. Then suddenly, before our eyes, there was a riot at the convention center and on the streets of Chicago. The news broadcasters were caught up in the melee and were getting beat up by the rioters. The rioters were savage, and the police were brutal. Mayor Daly's Chicago was in turmoil. 1968 had become the year of turmoil and rage.

Fast forward to the present.

On November 5, 2008, 40 years later, in the city of Chicago, Barack Obama gave his acceptance speech and acknowledged that he had been elected President of the United States. This was momentous. 40 years after the death of Dr. Martin Luther King Jr. and Robert Kennedy the nation had elected a multi-racial, African American as President. Here was the son of a black (African) Kenyan father and a white mother from Kansas who had been elected as President of the United States. What kind of odds would one give that with his multiracial background, which includes Native American ancestry, and his multicultural upbringing from Kansas, Honolulu and Jakarta that he could ever become the leader of the free world? As Barack Obama said in an interview, when his family gathered around the Thanksgiving table, "it is like a mini United Nations."

Watching his inauguration on my color TV set on January 20, 2009 was a momentous occasion, for me, and for our nation.

I believe it was a momentous occasion, as well, for my family and extended family. We are a family that includes whites and blacks. We have two adopted Asian children from China in our extended family and our present family ancestry includes Native Americans. We are Republicans and Democrats, the young and the old, the well educated and the barely educated. Some of us are gay and others are straight. Some are prosperous and there are those who struggle economically; we are blue collar workers and white collar workers and some are retired. But we are all family. Our family is a microcosm of our country.

Back in the 60s when my husband and I were just getting started with our advanced educations and married life I was not paying much attention to the Civil Rights. My vision was limited to only my experiences. It would take several decades and many more stories to tell you how I caught and adopted the vision for peace, social justice and equality for all people, far too many stories for the scope of this book.

Trinice and Todd's wedding July 1998

September 11, 2001—
A Day That Will Live In Infamy
(Written for the 9th anniversary of 9/11)

I was no longer the pastor at Greenville Baptist Church. I had resigned. My last Sunday was Memorial Day Week-end. I was in mourning during those early months of being "unemployed" and I was angry, frightened and feeling abandoned.

In spite of being depressed under those personal circumstances, it was an ordinary Tuesday. I went to my Smithfield Rotary meeting at the Kountry Kitchen in Greenville, RI. We always started promptly at 7 a.m. and broke at 8:30a.m. I don't recall who our speaker was for that day. I was the Chaplain of our chapter and I had offered a prayer of thanksgiving for a day to enjoy, another day to live out our motto "Service Above Self." The Rotarians have what is known as the Four-Way Test that asks the following questions:

Is it the TRUTH?
Is it FAIR to all concerned?
Will it build GOODWILL and BETTER FRIENDSHIPS?
Will it be BENEFICIAL to all concerned?

I was asked to join the Rotary Club three years prior. I was the Protestant clergy representative for this Service Club of business persons and entrepreneurs. I was thrilled to be in the Rotary because my Dad was a life-long member of Rotary. Prior to the acceptance of women into the Rotary, Dad voiced his concerns that women might not fit in. I can remember saying to him: "Well, at the country club where you meet, do they have a ladies room?" To which he replied, "yes." And I said, "Then when Rotary International accepts business women into their club, they will fit in because there are bathrooms for them." During the last years of Dad's life, we enjoyed going to Rotary together. He eventually became pleased that women were now a part of the organization and together we could share the camaraderie offered by this service group.

When our meeting was over and we had said our good-byes, I went to Agla's house on Douglas Circle, around the corner from Kountry Kitchen. I had a 10a.m. doctor's appointment and so instead of going back to the Lake House, I thought I could spend a little time with Agla. I arrived at just about 8:40. She was in her bathrobe and didn't mind at all that I had just "stopped by." She had been watching the *Today Show*. We said our pleasantries when suddenly there on the TV was a scene in which a commercial jet liner was crashing into one of the Twin Towers of the World Trade Center of New York. We were stunned! We simply did not understand how such an accident could happen. How could a plane fly into a building? Yet, there it was. The building was engulfed in flames and thick black smoke. I don't remember how many minutes later when another super jet flew into the other tower of the World Trade Center. Chaos was everywhere. People were running for their lives. You could see people jumping out of windows, bodies flying through the air to certain death. The buildings were engulfed in flames and smoke right before our eyes. Later the TV commentators would be shouting, almost incoherently, about planes being hijacked by Islamic fanatics. This was a deliberate terrorist attack on the United States, and on United States soil! Agla and I just clung to each other and wept. Then, we held hands and prayed. This was another day that would "Live in Infamy"!

Since I had to be in Providence, I needed some time to get there, so I left Alga's home and listened to the radio on my drive into Providence. By the time I was in the Dr.'s waiting room, I heard on the radio that another plane had hit the Pentagon and a fourth plane had gone down somewhere near Pittsburgh. That is all I knew then. "Somewhere near Pittsburgh" is where I grew up and where my brother and his wife and my Dad lived. A super jet liner had gone down, possibly on or near them. I was scared and worried for them. I needed to know where in the Pittsburgh area the plane had gone down.

Somehow my Dr. was able to attend to my care and we prayed together for our country and then I went home. I stayed glued to the TV set for the rest of the day, learning that the fourth plane had gone down in a field in Shanksville, PA. I had never heard of Shanksville,—my family was safe.

It was one of the worst days in American history. The worst attack on mainland America. It was an act of war. The United States responded to the attacks by launching a War on Terrorism, invading Afghanistan to depose the Taliban who had harbored al-Qaeda terrorists, and the USA Patriot Act enacted by Congress was put into place. Nine years later and we are still fighting and losing American lives in Afghanistan to keep America safe from terrorists!!

You, Dear Reader, can read in other sources about the complete devastation of the Twin Towns, the enormous number of causalities, the heroics of the firefighters and police in New York City. The world was stunned. Airports were closed. The stock market was closed. People were stranded in airports, unable to get home. Phyllis and I had tickets for a trip to Egypt sponsored by the Pittsburgh Theological Seminary. We were to leave that Friday. We canceled our trip! We needed to be home, near family and with the congregation at the Oak Lawn Baptist Church. When we arrived to worship on Sunday, September 16th the congregation was overjoyed to have their Pastor Phyllis with them and not in Egypt as planned.

What I want to share with you, Dear Reader, was my visit in early December, 2001 to New York City. The Reverend Dahler Hays, Executive Minister of the United Church of Christ of Rhode Island, had put together a trip for his RI clergy to go to New York. The economy of NYC had bottomed out, so one of his objectives for us was to go and show our solidarity with the people of NYC, by doing our "Christmas Shopping" there. The city was not a festive place. There were the usual holiday decorations, but the city was quiet, in mourning, covered in a cloud of dust, doubts, fear and depression. I did not shop. I couldn't.

Shopping was not the biggest nor the only objective of our trip. We had a scheduled meeting with The Reverend Dr. James Forbes, who was at that time, Senior Pastor of the Riverside Church. Dr. Forbes was able to speak to us about how his church and other churches responded to the crises, caring for the injured, helping people look for lost loved-ones, making sandwiches for the firefighters, making sacred space available to all who came to pray. He spoke of ways we could help to create a world where love took precedence over hate, where peace took precedence over war.

Then we went to "Ground Zero" this huge ugly hole. Dust was everywhere and covered everything. The smell of decaying bodies still hung in the air. The buildings surrounding the World Trade area were boarded up and many showed signs of severe damage. Rescue workers were still looking for the remains of the lost. Dust and debris was everywhere. There was a cyclone fence that encircled the area where once stood the Twin Towers. People left mementos at the fence. Photos, poems, prayers, a scarf, a fireman's helmet, a police badge, letters, ribbons, flowers, and countless other things were left as a tribute to the enormous loss of life that awful day. There are no words to describe how I felt standing at Ground Zero by the fence at the place where almost 3,000 lives were lost and over 6,000 people were injured at one time. We were as close to Ground Zero as one could get. Later, severe restrictions were put in place, and close-up access to the site was limited to official personnel.

We rode on the bus, back to Rhode Island, in silence. No one had any words of wisdom, comment or reflections. We were too stunned by the magnitude of the devastation and loss of life. It would take time.

Epilogue

Two years after the attack, I was visiting my family in Pennsylvania. After leaving my sister Nancy's home in Carlisle, PA, and traveling via the PA Turnpike, heading west to Pittsburgh, I decided that I had to visit Shanksville, the field where flight 93 went down on 9/ll. It is believed that this fourth plane was headed for the White House or at least Washington, DC, but some of its passengers and flight crew attempted to overcome the hijackers and retake control of the plane. In any event, the plane, with all passengers and crew aboard, crashed in this obscure field in central PA. I asked for directions and found the site. Where there was once a super jet liner imbedded in the ground, nose first and where everyone on the plane was killed, there was now, two years later, a beautiful green pasture. How still and beautiful this place was. I thought of the 23rd Psalm: "He maketh me to lie down in green pastures." There was no sign of the tragic loss of life and the hatred behind the hijackings of 9/11. There was a cyclone fence for mementos. Like NYC, there were poems and letters, photos, badges, firefighters helmets from around the country. There were mementoes from around the world. I left a tear stained, very wet handkerchief at Shanksville, just as I had left one at Ground Zero.

These were two pilgrimages I will never forget. I have not stopped to pray at the Pentagon, but I have driven by it. On September 11, 2008 President Bush uncovered a permanent memorial to those who died at the Pentagon where the third plane deliberately crashed. Some day there will be permanent memorials at Shanksville and Ground Zero for the world to see and remember. My heart carries a permanent memorial for all three sites.

Life has changed for all of us. Life was turned upside down that fateful, tragic day, and the repercussions are too many to write about in this short essay. As long as I have memory, I will never forget what I was doing and what was happening to our world between 8:42 and10: 30 a.m. on September 11, 200l.

Retirement
Or
How to Keep On Keeping On

Was it so long ago that I would hum and sing the words that Eddy Arnold would croon? "I don't want to set the world on fire. I just want to start a flame in your heart."

I did want to set the world on fire 30 years ago when I first started as Student Pastor at The Pendleton Hill Baptist Church. I had a fire burning in my heart to preach and teach, counsel and spread the gospel around the world. One learns a great deal after 30 years in the pulpit.

I've prepared and preached approximately 1200 sermons over the past 30 years. I can't remember, specifically, more than one or two favorites that have stood out in my mind. It is like being a mother. A mother fixes meals for 365 days a year, multiplied by, forever . . . and her family only remembers Thanksgiving, plus a few of her favorite recipes, and they will kindly remind her of the one recipe that was a total flop.

They never forget the flop. In fact, I don't think that one's children are particularly willing to forgive and forget their perceived childhood slights and insults which parents have cast upon them. "You weren't there for me when . . . ;" "You didn't allow me to do such and such . . . ;" "You were too strict or too lenient or too whatever." The big castigating reminder from my family is, "The church always came first." And they are accurate in that accusation. The pastoral ministry is never a 9-5 job. As hard as I tried to be present, emotionally and physically, on the home front, there were always nightly meetings to juggle along with ball practice and games, projects at school which needed help and the general taxi service that younger children require; all this as a single parent and as a pastor whose parishioners expected their pastor to be available, at least spiritually, 24/7. I confess that my family often got shortchanged! I feel badly about this because it is the family that deserves our very best and one expects them to be with you forever. Parishes come and go.

"I don't want to set the world on fire. I just want to start a flame in your heart."

I no longer try to set the world on fire. 30 years of institutional church reality and living in the reality of the world have dimmed my flame to some extent. The reality was—I spent much of my time in the parish putting out flames and fires which had the potential of consuming everyone, i.e. pastor and people. I am now content to just start a little flame in someone's heart about my love for Christ, His church and His mission.

Since this memoir is primarily about my life in the parish, the ups and downs, the joys and sorrows, starting flames of motivation and the dousing of fires of discontent, I will leave you with my reflections about those aspects of my life. This is not the avenue to explore and share with you my reflections on parenting, family, marital status, companionships or the great world problems.

The ancient theologian, Augustine, wrote about the visible and invisible church. The invisible church is the eternal church, the ideal, the unblemished concept of the universal church held in the mind of Christ. The visible church is merely a receptacle and often has nothing to do with the reality of the invisible church, but it has been developed as the icon of the invisible church over the centuries. The visible church has been responsible for much horror, death and destruction over the centuries . . . too numerous to list. The "Crusades" are a good example. You, Dear Reader, know of what I speak and you could give your own litany of your criticisms of the visible institutional church. Conversely, without the visible church the world would be deprived of much goodness, beauty, music, architecture, institutions of learning and healing, love, peace, comfort and joy to countless folk, whether they are proclaimed Christians or not! It has been my passion, for most of my life, to help build up the visible church and to assist and equip the Saints who worship, pray, work and serve within her midst. I use St. Paul's term "Saints" to include all followers of Christ.

The number one word of advice which I offer to those who would be "Saints" is PASSION. I would offer to anyone considering the pastorate or who is already embedded up to your neck in the nitty gritty work of parish life is this: You must have a passion for Christ, His church and His mission. I deliberately use the word passion, a word that Webster defines as "an emotion: intense, driving, or an overmastering feeling or conviction." Webster also defines "passion" as: "ardent affection: LOVE: a strong liking or desire for or devotion to some activity, object, or concept: sexual desire: an object of desire or deep interest." And I also use the word passion in the more obscure meaning of suffering as in the "Passion of Christ on the Cross"

It goes without saying that all who believe that they are called to the ordained ministry, must have a passion for the One whom they believed said, "Come, follow me." This passion for Christ is not always felt and understood by the people of the world, let alone those within one's immediate family. I cannot explain how one "knows" when Christ has called you to follow in His footsteps and to lead others to knowing and loving God, but you know! You know you can do nothing less but to try to live out His call. Through prayer, study of scripture, worship and service, I try to maintain a relationship with God through Christ. Like any human relationship, the more time you spend together, the better you come to understand the other and the other begins to understand you. I have tried to develop and maintain that relationship since I was a child, with the usual rebellions and reunions and with a mature steadfast commitment. If anyone does not have a passion for something, whether it be teaching or gardening or fishing or fighting for justice or healing, then that person may soon burn out, give up and perhaps quit. It is the passion, the drive, the overwhelming convictions I have about God, through Christ, that keep me going.

So I have a passion for Christ and what He symbolizes. I also have a passion for His church . . . the church as it is meant to be, i.e. the invisible church, the church that has the potential to be a healing, learning, loving, serving, worshipping community of believers. I have a deep love or passion for the people who make up the congregations within the churches that I have been asked to serve. I have tried to love and guide them into wholeness. I have tried to enable the members of the congregation to be "a church" in the healthiest manner possible for them at that time, in that place. Using the parenting analogy again: as a parent I want my children "to grow in wisdom and in stature and in favor with God and humankind"[27] and then when they are ready to stand on their own two feet I set them free. As a pastor I have tried to fix what is broken and mend up the brokenhearted and remind all parishioners that God loves them and so do I. Yet, as you know, this loving, leading, coaching, preaching, teaching doesn't always cast out the demons within the individual. And then, like Christ, the pastor has to endure the passion of suffering . . . suffering with, and suffering for . . . the church!

I have a passion for Christ's "mission", articulated best, for me, by Jesus when he returned to his home town of Nazareth and read from the book of Isaiah during the Sabbath service:

> *'The Spirit of the Lord is upon me,*
> *because he has anointed me*
> *to bring good news to the poor.*
> *He has sent me to proclaim release to the captives*
> *and recovery of sight to the blind,*
> *to let the oppressed go free,*
> *to proclaim the year of the Lord's favor.'*[28]

Christ's mission has to be my mission. Those who are rich in material things are often the poorest of souls when it comes to the standards of the Kingdom of God. When our group from the Rhode Island American Baptist Churches, which included members of Greenville Baptist Church, went to the Dominican Republic in the early 1990s I had never before been in such a poor country. I thought that sections of West Virginia, where I went to college, and Mexico, where I studied for a time, were poor, but I came to realize that they were rich beyond belief compared to the Haitian population living in LaRoma, Dominican Republic. These people had practically nothing—materially. Most lived on sugar cane plantations like squatters in make-shift shacks. They were born on the plantation and they died there. They lived in mud huts and subsided on sugar cane and a few fruits and vegetables they could beg or buy with their very meager earnings. In spite of this abject material poverty, I never met a group of more cheerful souls.

---

[27] Luke 2:40 NRSV

[28] Luke 4:18-19 NRSV Isaiah 61: 1-2

During their worship services they sang and danced to drum music, seemingly without a care in the world. They had a passion for God unlike anyone or any group of people I had ever met before or since! In their own way, and through their joy and happiness, they preached the good news of Christ to the poor of Rhode Island, i.e. the American Baptists! We brought money, clothes, medicines, and the willingness to help build a hospital for these Haitian workers, but our faith and our joy could not compare to their faith and their joy, living as they were, in the most despicable living and working conditions.

I have never been involved in a prison ministry, but I believe that many people have been wrongfully imprisoned and need to be set free: perhaps the DNA tests will be a 21st Century instrument of justice.

Imprisonment means other things. We see people who have been imprisoned by bad habits and addictions, imprisoned by grudges, imprisoned by the desire for revenge, imprisoned by hatred and by discrimination, imprisoned by poverty, imprisoned by poor education and poor health, and imprisoned by hunger. I have spent these past 30 years trying to release these captives from their bondage. It has been my mission to help motivate the congregations that I have served to take this mission of Christ seriously and encourage them to help release the captives. The only way to operate in this mission field of releasing the captives is with the help of the Holy Spirit. We need the Spirit's help to correct our blindness so that our eyes are opened to the needs of our neighbors near and far. All Christians need to ask that we be given the eyes of faith to see the needs of those around us, those whom we can serve in the name of the Christ.

There are the oppressed living next door who need to be set free from the bondage of depression, and we may not even know it. Domestic violence is not limited to time, place, race, color or social status. There are people oppressed by life sucking-marriages who need spiritual and material guidance and the ways and means and, often, the courage to be set free. There are parents struggling with their roles, some with ungrateful children, some with spoiled children, and some with children with special needs, and all parents, I think, need to be released from the oppressive media model of the "perfect parenting." Most parents do the best they can with what they have to work with at the time. The nations need to be set free from the oppression of war. The world longs for Peace and yet we have no idea how to go about finding peace. We have the Naval War College here in Rhode Island, but where is the Academy for Peace?

When I speak and preach about peace, I am talking about far more than the absence of war. I like the connotations found in the Hebrew word SHALOM. Shalom is a form of greeting and a form of saying good-by. Shalom means far more than a salutation or just the absence of war. Shalom is a wish on the part of the speaker that means wholeness, prosperity, safety, completeness, health, welfare, soundness, tranquility, perfection, rest, harmony, as well as the absence of agitation or discord. So in essence, when I speak out the word *SHALOM* as a blessing—I am not only proclaiming peace but all the above meanings of the word over that person—that's a mighty blessing!!!

For my closing reflections, now in my early retirement from active ministry, I do have a word of advice as a pastor and a retired pastor for "How To Keep On Keeping On" offered to your Dear Reader. You may be a pastor, a retired pastor, a family member or friend, or a Christian in any walk of life. I would like to quote St. Paul, in his epistle to the church in Philippi, who gives us the clues.[29]

1. **Rejoice in the Lord always. Again I say rejoice! "Celebrate God all day, every day. I mean revel in him!"**

Dear Reader, this is the great secret of and for a fulfilled life. If you love God with heart, soul, mind and strength . . . you really can't be without joy in your life. Yes, there are going to be hills and valleys in every life, but for consistent joy in living, every day, if you follow Christ's mission, you will experience perpetual joy. In every parish that I have served we have spent an enormous amount of time laughing, loving and serving together. We found joy in one another through the Lord. We must always pray for those who have become so doleful that they have forgotten how to laugh, or know joy. (I understand that joy and laughter are not interchangeable, but I don't see one without the other.)

Back in 2005 I had to provide an intake evaluation at the cardiac rehab center. There were countless questions and forms about my health, etc. Then there was a series of blocks to check as to what I thought I needed help with: fatigue, weight management, diabetes control and a little check box with the letters S.O.B. following it. Was I being asked if I qualify as an s.o.b? I looked at the nurse and said, "Well it depends on

[29] Phil. 4: 1-9, The Message, Eugene Peterson.

whom you ask if I qualify as an S.O.B. Some say, yes and some say no." She just looked at me, then she pondered for a moment and then laughed and said, "S.O.B. stands for Shortness of Breath; you don't need help."

2. **"Have no anxiety" or as the KJV reads: Be careful of nothing. Eugene Peterson's, translation *The Message* reads, "Don't fret or worry".**

Jesus told his disciples about freedom from worry long before Paul preached it. You will remember from the Bible: "Therefore, I tell you, do not be anxious about your life, what you shall eat or what you shall drink, nor about your body, what you shall put on . . . But first seek His kingdom and righteousness, and all these things shall be yours. Therefore do not be anxious about tomorrow, for tomorrow will be anxious for itself. Let the day's trouble be sufficient for the day."[30] Good advice for all of us after these exhausting years and months watching our economy spin out of control.

It does seem that the more material things that we have, the more we worry. And it is a funny thing how a $100 dollar bill seems like such a huge amount when we donate it to the church, but such a small amount when we go shopping!

As I wrote above, the most joyful and carefree people I ever met were a group of Baptist Christians living in poverty in the Dominican Republic. Their joy, their faith, their commitment to living the gospel of Jesus Christ put my own faith to shame.

3. **"If you have to fret and worry, do it through prayer". Actually Paul's words are to remind us to pray honestly. Let God know what is on your heart and mind.**

I suspect there are some readers who are not prayer warriors. Perhaps we fear looking to God as if God were some sort of heavenly Santa Claus, and we do not ask for things because it seems so greedy. Some people aren't convinced about this thing called prayer. We aren't sure it works. Some folk are angry that prayers have been ignored . . . God seems so distant. Some are too angry at God to pray—they have been disappointed in the

[30] Matthew 6: 25-33

past. All these thoughts and feelings are okay; in fact these thoughts are classic spiritual inquiries. Read the psalms. See how the psalmist wrestled with these very thoughts: i.e. the distance of God, anger toward God, unanswered prayer and so forth. A simple statement addressed to God is sufficient:

- "teach me to pray, Lord." Or
- "I am too angry to pray, God." Or
- "I believe, help my unbelief."
- Just be honest in your prayer life!

4. Say thank you. Mean thank you. A gracious life is a life of being thankful.

Burnout can be a real thing at church: Spiritual burnout, emotional burnout and even physical burnout. This is true as well in business, teaching, home-making, care-giving, etc. When someone says, "Thank you" it can mean so much; it is not only graciousness, it is empowerment, music to the soul, the balm of Gilead. I sent hand written cards to express my thanks to the members of the congregation. I thanked them for a particular service or gift or luncheon or birthday or condolences received at the time of a death. I took the opportunity to say thank you often and sincerely. In return I have received countless notes of appreciation over the years. It means so much to know that you and your efforts are appreciated. When you say "thank you" it will be a soothing balm to others, the sunshine when life seems dreary and dark.

5. and finally, carry on. Keep on keeping on.

Continue in whatever things that you do and think about, Dear Reader, that are honorable, just, pure, lovely, gracious, excellent, and are praiseworthy . . . keep on keeping on. The God of peace will be with you. SHALOM

Forever Friends Phyllis and Lynne

Acknowledgements

I have had the wonderful pleasure of working with Charles Nardone, Esq. He was the first reader and "editor" of this work. He has tirelessly worked on the manuscript and has made my writing better!! During this time of writing and rewriting, Charlie has always been helpful and he laughs at my jokes . . . so of course I love him.

I offer my thanks to Jo-Ellen Fisher, a Master educator, English teacher, proof reader, copy editor and my friend. She took the time to truly study, search, scrutinize, and sanitize my writing skills.

This memoir would not have happened without the Memoir Writers Group on Block Island, Rhode Island. A heartfelt thank you to Edith Blane, Eleanor Garrett, Sandra Greenman, Ellen Jacke and Martha Wilson for your patient listening, gentle suggestions and allowing me to periodically return from the Main Land, known to you as America, to join in such good fun and company.

Knowing I would miss my Block Island memoirists I offered to facilitate a Memoirs Writing Group at the Oak Lawn Community Baptist Church. Thank you to the Reverend Phyllis E. Hackett, Pastor Emerita of Oak Lawn Community Baptist Church for your support and love, your words of encouragement; you are my love, my peace and my joy. Thank you to Mary Ackroyd, Steven Kemp, Diane (Dee) Kolb, Vivian Fanning, Helen Richards, Francis Sission, and Charles (Chuck)Wales,

My sisters, Nancy Bowermaster and Martha Caughey encouraged me to pursue this endeavor after reading the first rough draft of Part One and Two. Thank you for your kind words, your encouragement and your love. Thank you family! I hold you in my heart. Forgive me when I was not able to be present to you as you needed and wanted over these years. Brother, Ted Caughey and his wife Dolly, brother-in-law, Dave Bowermaster, my children Todd Holden and his beautiful wife Trinice and their sons Robert and Mark and my lovely daughter, Rebecca Collins and her sons, Lance and Isaac. And forever, Phyllis. Thank you all!

Finally, I give my love and gratitude to the many fellow Christian companions who have accompanied me on this extraordinary journey. May God's love, peace and joy always attend to your ways,